YVES DJIKI

They were born of God

Revelation of the New Creation

To the Lord of Glory Jesus Christ,
Who knew me before the foundation of the world and who leads
my steps.
Thank you for revealing the profound things of God.

Psalm 82 verse 6 to 7; KJV

6 I have said, Ye are gods; and all of you are children of the most High. 7 But ye shall die like men, and fall like one of the princes.

Is it possible that we did not understand God's intention when he chose to create man in his image and likeness? (Genesis 1 verses 26 to 27)

Can man really rise above what is common to walk in the dimension of God?

Contents

Preface

Dear readers,

Driven by the Holy Spirit, I sought to comprehend why the experiences of most Christians differed greatly from those of Jesus and the individuals who walked with God. If God is the same yesterday, today, and forever, the reason for the lack of power must be found on the side of man.

They were born of God summarizes some of the key elements that we have discovered in recent years of researching and putting into practice revelations about the New Creation . The Word of God is established in heaven forever. Today as yesterday, he wants to be strong in the lives of his children. I pray that this book will take you further in your quest for excellence in Jesus. Those who believe in Him are granted the privilege to carry out His works (John 14:12).

By browsing these pages, you will discover, in chapter 1, the extraordinary dream of God, who created man to live in the dimension of God.

Chapter 2 is about Christian identity. Man is what he thinks. If the image we have of ourselves is below what God says about us, we will be limited. The purpose of this chapter is to destroy the lies we have believed about ourselves. Jesus became all that we were so that we could become all that he is. It is the revelation of our union with Jesus that is the source of our strength.

Chapter 3 reminds us that the normal Christian life is supernatural. Jesus is the model who comes down from heaven. Copying it is the path to success. Key elements are given in this chapter to facilitate understanding of the model and its implementation.

Chapter 4 is a collection of testimonies aimed at showing how merciful and faithful God is. Here, we will discover that it does not make a difference among men. Whoever allows himself to be led will see the glory of God. The ardent desire to possess the things he gives opens the doors of his grace.

Chapter 5 is a collection of prayers, devotion, and authority to help everyone achieve victories in various fields. They are prayer models to rely on to go further.

At the end of the book are the steps you need to take to become a Christian. The proclamation of the Cross must lead to the repentance of those affected. One must be immersed in the waters in the name of Jesus. And the Father is going to clothe him with the Holy Spirit.

This book is addressed to all men, especially those who would like to experience God's supernatural way in a natural way.

It is the privilege of the sons of God to walk like God.

I hope you enjoy reading and I pray that this book meets your expectations. I pray that the Holy Spirit will light a fire that will inspire you to go even further into the profound things of God.

Be richly blessed in the name of Jesus Christ,

Yves Djiki

Acknowledgments

The realization of this project would not have been possible without the participation of several people whom I would like to recognize and thank.

I thank the Holy Spirit, my senior partner, who has been with me every step, advising me on the choice of ideas and structure.

I thank my family members, especially my wife, Bénédicte, for your unwavering support, intercession, patience, wise advice, and valuable feedback. Together, we form a winning team. To my children, Jérémie-Benel, Raphaël-Joshua, Isaïe-Nathan, and Ely Danielle; to my sons Dave, Patrick, and William, thank you for your encouragement and understanding throughout this project.

I thank the *Église Vie pour Christ* family from Canada, Cameroon, and the world for your love and support. It was by serving among you that the Lord Jesus formed me. And it continues to polish me through the blessed interactions we have.

I thank the intercession team of the *Église Vie pour Christ* in Montreal for the fervent prayers raised every day, not only for the success of this project but for all the things that the Father has placed in me.

Thanks to Olivier and Liliane, Nathalie, Lionel, Dave, and Isaïe-Nathan for the precious testimonies of God's fidelity in their lives. This project would not have achieved its goal without your contributions, which will bless many people.

Thanks to all the reviewers: Bénédicte, Ely Danielle, Dave, Lionel, Jules, Olivier, Liliane, and Joyce, for your valuable feedback on the first versions of the manuscript. Your constructive criticism has greatly improved this book.

Finally, thank you to everyone who believes in us. Your presence at our side, your encouragement, your prayers, and your multifaceted support are greatly appreciated.

1

God's extraordinary dream

The Big Why

A being who is in the image and likeness of God walks the earth as the representative of God.

Clothed in the Spirit of God, his justice, and his glory, Adam, the first man, ruled the earth until the terrible day when he abandoned his position as a son of God and lord of the earth.

Until then, he had lived in communion with God, who visited the Garden of Eden every evening. He had participated in God's work by giving a name to each of the animals that God had created.

Adam's mandate was simple: to cultivate and care for the garden and to ensure that those who would come after him complied with the Words of God that had been revealed.

Eden is a place where God shows His presence in a special way. The scriptures speak of another Eden, where Lucifer was planted by the Lord to keep his glory and magnify his greatness. Because of the iniquity that was found in him, Lucifer was cast out of heaven (Ezekiel 28 verses 13 to 14).

He who had left heaven with a third of the angels could not bear to see Adam enjoy in a new Eden the privileges that were once his. This is how he came up with the idea of interrupting the idyll of the man who was the protector of God's glory and his representative on earth.

Genesis 3 tells the details of the temptation of the adversary and the fall of Adam. What is remarkable about the account of this dark tragedy is the hope aroused by God's promise: the descendants of the snake and that of the woman will be forever at war. Victory will belong to the seed of the woman (Genesis 3 verse 15).

How does the Lord speak of the woman's seed when we know that in the process of procreation, the seed comes from the man and the egg comes from the woman? By this, the Holy Spirit showed that the One who was to come would be different from other men.

God's outlandish love and his dream of living in communion with man will ensure that he visits Earth as a man to lift up man who had become in the image and likeness of the devil.

Therefore, the New Creation is God's long-hidden plan, initially prophesied by God himself in the Garden of Eden, taken up by numerous prophets who spoke on His behalf, and implemented by God Himself when he visited the earth (1 Timothy 3 verse 16).

Since Jesus Christ, a new race of men has been walking on Earth. They are no longer slaves to death and sin. Satan no longer has any authority over them. They are sons of God and participate in his kingdom and glory.

Preparation time

It begins immediately after the publication of God's judgment on the protagonists of the rebellion: Satan, Adam, and Eve.

Created to live in communion with God, Adam and Eve did not have to rely on their own experience to know good and evil. As sons of God, they had to depend entirely on His Spirit.

Now that they were spiritually dead (separated from Him, who is the Source of all true life), they needed to be preserved from eternal condemnation. Angels were posted to the east of the garden, from which Adam and Eve had just been expelled. Access to the Tree of Life had to be protected (Genesis 3 verses 22 to 24).

The first sacrifices appear in Genesis 4 with Abel and Cain

(Genesis 4 verses 3 to 4). The Holy Spirit's comment on Abel's accepted sacrifice because of his faith shows that Jehovah showed them how to worship and how to commune with God through altars and sacrifices.

Seth—substituted: this is what the name of Adam's third son means; he is the one that Yahweh gives in place of Abel, whom Cain killed. The truth is that the devil did not want to see the One Who was foretold appear.

Seth gave birth to Enosch, and it is said that men began to invoke the name of God on earth. The Hebrew term translated "to invoke" means to approach a person you meet, to call by name, to proclaim, to invite, or to pronounce.

God will send the flood to purify the earth from the corruption with which the devil planned to thwart the coming of the seed of women. Fallen angels had mated with women, and a race of demonic hybrids was walking and destroying the earth.

From the eight that had been saved through the waters, the whole earth was populated. About 2200 years after the promise made in the garden, Yahweh chose to make a covenant with a man (Abraham). His coming to earth was to be through a people that he chose and established as the light of the world (Isaiah 49 verses 3 and 6).

After 430 years as slaves in Egypt, God transported them across the Red Sea and the desert to settle them in the land he had given as an inheritance to Abraham, his friend, and their father.

God also gave them the law and the prophets so that they might learn his ways. Through the Tabernacle and all the ceremonies, through the observation of the feasts, the people prophetically repeated various aspects of the ministry of the Lamb of God.

A multitude of prophets prophesied, saying: He will come; he will remove our faults; he will do everything new. When the time had come, John, the greatest of all the prophets, seemed to say: He is in your midst—repent.

The need for the new birth

Jesus said to the first disciples who followed him: "And he saith unto him, Verily, verily, I say unto you, Hereafter ye shall see heaven open, and the angels of God ascending and descending upon the Son of man." (John 1 verse 51; KJV).

The open sky and angels ascending and descending refer to the vision that Jacob had that special night spent in Bethel— the place where his grandfather Abraham once built an altar to Yahweh. Jacob was near a gate of heaven, and he did not know it (Genesis 12 verse 8; 28 verses 11 to 17).

The Son of Man—this expression reflects the fact that he partook of flesh and blood to become the next kin of man. Only a close relative has the right to buy back a family mem- ber. Through the prophet Daniel's vision, we understand that he is the One whom the Ancient of Days established over everything—the ANOINTED (Daniel 7 verses 13 to 14).

In the past, Yahweh manifested his glorious presence in the places where altars were built, especially in the Tabernacle and the temple. In the New Creation, he longs to make man the place of his presence.

The Lamb of God was therefore the model for the mobile tabernacles that the Father intended to build. In Spirit, they would form a spiritual house in which Jesus would be both the foundation and the head.

To Nicodemus, the leader of the Jews who came to see him at night to be taught about the doctrine of Christ, Jesus insisted on the need for a new birth (John 3, verses 3 to 8). Those who descended from Adam are in the image and likeness of Adam: he was spiritually dead, and so are they.

All the moral education that man can receive to be good to his neighbor does not change his profound nature, which is that of the devil. The very fact that he lives as he pleases is proof that he is a rebel (Ephesians 2 verses 1 to 5).

In regard to the miracles and wonders that accompanied His ministry, Jesus Christ said that it was the Father who dwelt in Him who did them (John 14 verse 20). It is through the Holy Spirit that the Father does work on earth.

The Holy Spirit had been with everyone who walked and spoke in the name of God on earth. He was also alongside the disciples when they cast out demons in the name of Jesus. Since they were not yet alive, he could not be in them as he was in Jesus.

That is why Jesus made this glorious promise to them when he spoke to them about the necessity for his death and resurrection, as well as about the coming of the Holy Spirit: he abides with you, and he will be in you (John 14 verse 17). And immediately after, for I live, and you will also live (John 14 verse 18).

Because I live, and you will also live: it is important to understand that the New Covenant inaugurated by Jesus through his death on the cross only really came into full operation with the descent of the Holy Spirit on the day of Pentecost. Thus, Jesus did his earthly ministry primarily under the Old Covenant. His followers were not born again.

The Holy Spirit went with the disciples sent by Jesus, as he went with the prophets sent by Yahweh. He could only stand by their side. For Jesus, who was sinless, the Holy Spirit descended on Him the day he was immersed in the waters of the Jordan River.

He abides with you, and he will be in you; the sequence we see in the scriptures is this: the Father builds the Tabernacle according to the model he sets. And he sends his Spirit to live there when all things are put in their place and sanctified. This is also what we are seeing with the construction of the Jerusalem Temple. His glory comes when the construction is finished and everything is in its place.

Through the miracle of the new birth, the Holy Spirit builds the house in which he comes to live. You have to be born again.

For the disciples, this miracle occurred on the evening of the Resurrection, when the God who had breathed the spirit of life into the tent where Adam was to live, breathed on the disciples gathered in the upper room (John 20, verses 21 to 22). The Spirit who gives power would come upon them about 49 days later—on the day of Pentecost.

Entering the dimension of God

The march of the Church is like that of the Israelites, who were delivered from slavery in Egypt. After being baptized into Moses in the sea and in the cloud and seeing his glory through various miracles, the majority perished in the desert (1 Corinthians 10 verses 1 to 5).

They did not enter Canaan because they were full of Egypt. Those who walked with the Lord of Heavenly Hosts continued to think like slaves.

Although it's hard for us to recognize it, we are greatly influenced by what we think and believe. Our life is the fruit of our thoughts. Life and death are in the power of the tongue (Proverbs 18 verse 21). Considering that our words reflect the abundance of our hearts, we are indeed primarily accountable for our circumstances.

The new birth, the immersion in water, and the immersion in the Holy Spirit are no guarantee that we will walk in the dimension of God. Until we are transformed by the renewal of our intelligence, we will remain in the *desert of the world.*

Many people are frustrated and confused by the fact that they are not seeing God's promises fulfilled in their lives. Sometimes we say, "God thought it was good not to give me this or that" when talking about the things that are covered by redemption. Which, of course, is far from the truth. Indeed, the scriptures say that he blessed us with all kinds of spiritual blessings in heavenly places.

Spiritual knowledge is what we need; each of us is always one revelation away from a breakthrough.

By baptizing the Israelites in Moses, in the sea, and in the cloud, the Lord placed them in the spiritual position of Moses, to whom He had revealed himself in the burning bush. They were offered the privilege of seeing God face-to-face, hearing his voice, living in his presence, etc.

Similarly, by baptizing us in the name of Jesus and giving us the gift of his Spirit, the Father placed us in the spiritual position of Jesus. We are as he is. We are children of God. We are offered the extraordinary privilege of doing the works that Jesus did and more (John 14 verse 12).

In the first case, as in the second, the ability to enjoy the privilege that the Lord gives depends on understanding the ways of God. Whoever does not know his God, whoever does not know who he is, and what he has received, will lose his reward.

What understanding do we have of the work of the cross? Have we understood that his death on the cross is our death? Have we understood that his resurrection is our resurrection? Adam's spirit was separate from Yahweh's. **Our spirit is ONE with the living God** (1 Corinthians 6 verse 17).

It is through His Spirit and for Him that we live. So we no longer know anyone according to the flesh (2 Corinthians 5 verse 16). We understand that a new and greater reality has taken place within us. It is through our commitment to recognize what is and to excel in using the tools that the Father has put at our disposal that we possess the kingdom.

In the chapters that follow, we present some aspects of what Jesus did for us from before the foundation of the world, and particularly at the Cross, until he sat at the right hand of God in heaven.

2

The identity of the Christian

John 1 verses 19 to 23; KJV

19 And this is the record of John, when the Jews sent priests and Levites from Jerusalem to ask him, Who art thou? 20 And he confessed, and denied not; but confessed, I am not the Christ. 21 And they asked him, What then? Art thou Elias? And he saith, I am not. Art thou that prophet? And he answered, No. 22 Then said they unto him, Who art thou? that we may give an answer to them that sent us. What sayest thou of thyself? 23 He said, I am the voice of one crying in the wilderness, Make straight the way of the Lord, as said the prophet Esaias.

Can he who does not know who he is really fulfill the mandate for which he came to earth?

The scriptures proclaim that without vision (revelation, knowl-edge), the people are relentless; they perish.

All men who have done something significant in the scriptures have been able to do so because Jehovah revealed their identity to them.

To Abram, with whom he made a covenant, he took him from Mesopotamia to Canaan and changed his name to "Abraham". He who had no son became the father of a multitude and the ancestor of Jesus.

To Moses, who cared for his father-in-law's sheep, the Lord told him that he was the one who would lead the people out of Egypt. The time had come to fulfill the promise of freedom made to Abraham 430 years earlier.

To Peter, Jesus will say: From now on, you will fish for men; feed my sheep...

To Saul, he said something along these lines. : You are an instrument that I have chosen to bear my name before the nations, before the kings, and before the sons of Israel (Acts 1 verse 15).

To all the apostles and to the Church, Jesus said: Go and make disciples of all nations... (Matthew 28 verse 18). We are all apostolos (envoys).

Whoever knows who he is will be confident enough to move

forward. His motivation will come from the fire that is within him through the vision he has received from God. His life shall have purpose, and through God's grace, he will receive all the strength needed to accomplish his role in God's work.

Christian identity is a concept that covers who he is in Jesus, what he has, and also what he is capable of doing.

Could the feelings of insecurity, inferiority, and confusion that many experience be attributed to the identity crisis they are facing?

Can someone who has poor self-esteem and is imprisoned by a distorted image of himself really develop healthy relationships with others? How can someone who feels bad about himself because he doesn't love himself be able to love others? How will he be able to meet the emotional needs of his spouse? How will he be able to positively influence his children?

Anyone who does not know who they are and what they have in Jesus is unable to project themselves into the future. He does not have the strength and confidence to dream of big things. Man will still be limited by what he thinks. Whoever thinks that he is nothing, that he does not have anything, and that he cannot go through life like a loser.

Conversely, whoever understands that he is a wonderful creature and that he came into this world to do great things, will rise up to do them.

> **Psalm 82 verses 6 to 7; KJV**
>
> 6 I have said, Ye are gods; and all of you are children of the most High. 7 But ye shall die like men, and fall like one of the princes.

It is in God that the truth about man's identity is found. If Adam's sin condemned man to live under the dominion of death and sin, the sacrifice of the Cross gives him the authority to become a child of God (Romans 7 verses 17 to 18, John 1 verses 12 to 13).

ONE is too small to do great things. It is not good for a man to be alone. God brings man into His dimension by uniting him with Jesus. It is in Him that man is perfected (Colossians 2 verse 10).

It is by examining the verses that contain expressions such as "In Him," "In Christ," "In Jesus," "With Him," and "Through Him." that we discover the identity and heritage of the Christian.

In Jesus

Sitting together in heavenly places

Ephesians 2 verse 6; KJV

And hath raised us up together, and made us sit together in heavenly places in Christ Jesus:

To his son Jesus Christ, who is the apostle of the New Covenant, the Father said: The LORD said unto my Lord, Sit thou at my right hand, until I make thine enemies thy footstool. (Psalm 110 verse 1; KJV). It was after his resurrection and ascension that the Father glorified him in this way.

Mark 16 verse 19; KJV

So then after the Lord had spoken unto them, he was received up into heaven, and sat on the right hand of God.

All power in heaven and on earth is in his hands. In this highly elevated position, Jesus is seated with those who believe in Him. In fact, he is not separated from the Church, which is his body.

If we could understand that our union with Jesus puts us above all else, we would continually raise our praise. Indeed, we share his reign and his glory. Those who have come back to life walk on snakes and scorpions. Death and sin no longer rule over them. They are in the dimension of God.

He who is seated is the king of all realms. Those who sit with Him are also kings. The sitting position is that of rest and also that of the Judge. Those who are seated dominate through the decrees that they issue by the Holy Spirit in various earthly and spiritual spheres.

What do we do with the authority he has given us? Do we know that he made a promise to establish the things we declare?

Job 22 verse 28; KJV

Thou shalt also decree a thing, and it shall be established unto thee: and the light shall shine upon thy ways.

We are sitting in the victory of Jesus. We are not confused. We know how it ends because everything was done at the cross at Golgotha. Whoever resists God's purposes will be put to flight. If we remain subject to the Spirit of God and offer the rebel good resistance, he will be defeated. We know how that ends.

Let's learn how to rest. The sitting position is that of rest.

Salvation is in calm and trust. There is tranquility in faith; an assurance that comes from the power of God to cover and carry us. We know that he sits on the throne and that he rules. We know that we are in his hands. We know that he came before us. Hallelujah.

Created for good works

Ephesians 2 verse 10; KJV

For we are his workmanship, created in Christ Jesus unto good works, which God hath before ordained that we should walk in them.

Just as Jesus was the visible representation of the invisible God, so is the Christian a visible representation of Jesus. In Antioch, they were first called by the initially pejorative name "Christian"—to say mockingly: look at these people who are embalmed of the doctrine of Christ.

The ultimate goal of the work he does in us is for us to be dispensers of God's life in the same way that Jesus was faithful during his earthly mission. We know that we are on the right track when the world sees more and more Jesus in us.

What are the good works that he has prepared, if not those that exalt and magnify his Name. He wants to be recognized as God by everyone. He would like to confirm the message we are announcing.

Let us not resist the call for repentance. The altars of Baal must be brought down if we want to see the glory of God. His word should take up all the space. Our lives ought not to be molded by the world's doctrines and philosophies. Jesus is the model we copy. Whoever wants to please men has abandoned Christ.

Galatians 1 verse 10; KJV

For do I now persuade men, or God? or do I seek to please men? for if I yet pleased men, I should not be the servant of Christ.

The Father has made everything new. He is the One who works in us through his Spirit. Let us therefore refrain from seeking within ourselves or in the world the means to establish the things that he entrusts to us. It is from Him that all our resources will come—yes, he uses men and the world. Let us leave the initiative to Him so as not to waste time.

Abraham's Blessing Participants

Galatians 3 verses 13 to 14; KJV

13 Christ hath redeemed us from the curse of the law, being made a curse for us: for it is written, Cursed is every one that hangeth on a tree: 14 That the blessing of Abraham might come on the Gentiles through Jesus Christ; that we might receive the promise of the Spirit through faith.

Abraham put his trust in God, who had promised him an offspring, and this was brought to justice. Abraham's name is exalted due to the One who descended from him.

Jesus is the source of blessing for all nations. Thus, at the cross, Jesus was made sin so that the curse of the law would be removed from us and so that we would receive justification by faith.

God sees neither iniquity nor sin in the life of the one who has put his trust in the work of the cross. He sees only the perfection of Jesus. Therefore, God gives whoever believes in Jesus the privilege of inheriting with Him. They are not farther away because of sin. They are sons of God and of the house of God. The Holy Spirit dwells in them, and they have God's powerful angels as companions in service.

This is Abraham's blessing that is offered to all of Adam's descendants.

Many will be delivered from the power of darkness and will come to life if the Lamb of God finds in us a well-established and powerfully active portal.

Have we resolved to follow the path set before us? Generational curses cannot restrain us if we open ourselves to guidance from the Holy Spirit. He will know how to find the roots to be pulled out. Just give Him our whole heart.

In Him

Enriched in all utterance and in all knowledge

1 Corinthians 1 verse 5; KJV

That in everything ye are enriched by him, in all utterance, and in all knowledge;

It is of paramount importance that we understand that it was as our representative that Jesus walked the earth. It was also in this capacity that he went to the cross to pay the price of our freedom from the devil's jails and our promotion into the position of sons of God, with all the advantages that come with that glorious rank. He is currently standing in the sky as our representative.

So everything he did was credited to us. What he got was also put into our account. We are joint heirs with Him.

The expression "enriched in all utterance" refers to all of God's promises—small, great, and precious.

The expression "enriched in all knowledge" refers to the work done in us through the revelation that we have of God's promises and their fulfillment in Jesus.

The paradox and tragedy of the Christian is to live in defeat like ordinary men when he has been filled with all the wealth of heaven in Jesus Christ. He perishes because he does not have the revelation of the truth.

The good news that we proclaim to all is that the Father has chosen to give all those whom he has placed in Jesus all the wealth of his glory. "Yes" and "Amen" are spoken in his name by his representatives on earth.

2 Corinthians 1 verse 19 to 20; KJV

19 For the Son of God, Jesus Christ, who was preached

among you by us, even by me and Silvanus and Timotheus, was not yea and nay, but in him was yea. 20 For all the promises of God in him are yea, and in him Amen, unto the glory of God by us.

We are the righteousness of God

2 Corinthians 5 verse 21; KJV

For he hath made him to be sin for us, who knew no sin; that we might be made the righteousness of God in him.

Justification is God's system by which he examines and places the stamp "Approved" on a man's life. The Holy Spirit speaks of Abraham, affirming that his trust in God was credited to him as righteousness. (Genesis 15 verses 5 to 7).

On a natural level, for Abram and Sarai, as they advanced in age, the idea of having offspring was an impossibility. They had to believe in Yahweh's ability and receive.

Man is in the same position. The idea of emancipation from slavery, death, sin, and the limitations of the flesh is an impossibility. Don't we often hear the expression "I'm just a man"? The God of Heaven has provided a means by which man can pass from death to life.

Jesus was made to be a curse by the Father on the cross in our stead. On Him have been laid our sin, our diseases, our curses, our weakness, our unworthiness, and everything that degrades us. This is so that we may become the righteousness of God.

The Holy Spirit, who had been forced to leave Adam on that terrible day when the image and likeness of God were replaced by the image and likeness of the rebellious snake, had waited for many years for the conditions for his return to be fulfilled.

The whole of heaven had lived with great frenzy when he was born in Bethlehem. His immersion in the waters of the Jordan River and the coming down of the Holy Spirit were also occasions of great joy—everything was happening as per God's initial plan. Another man was walking on earth, filled with the power of God, once again possessing his image and likeness.

The last Adam would be the head of a new house that the father was building. He had announced it in the garden and later through his prophets.

It is in a glorious explosion that the Holy Spirit will have the joy of descending on the approximately 120 disciples who were in the upper room that Sunday morning, which followed the Ascension of our Lord. Later that same day, 3,000 people joined God's family. All were according to the pattern that comes down from heaven—recreated in Him and filled with his Spirit.

He to whom the justice of Jesus is attributed is no longer in the image of Adam, who was driven out of the garden. He is like Jesus, who is without blemish before God.

We have become heirs of God

> **Ephesians 1 verse 11; KJV**
>
> In whom also we have obtained an inheritance, being predestinated according to the purpose of him who worketh all things after the counsel of his own will.

The Father formed the project of making us his children. This resolution, which remained hidden from the powers and authorities, was masterfully implemented in the death and resurrection of Jesus Christ.

Everything that the Father has, the Son also has. Whatever the Father does, the Son also does (John 5, verses 19-20); John 10 verse 38). Because we are ONE Spirit with Jesus (1 Corinthians 6:17), we participate in the kingdom and glory of God.

The parable of the father who refuses to make his rebellious son an ordinary worker but who chooses to treat him as a king shows the heart of God to the repentant sinner (Luke 15 verses 20 to 24). He who is born of God is the son of God. He exercises authority in the domain of the Father. Everything that the Father has also belongs to him. He can relish it as he pleases, for he is cherished by his father, who can deny him nothing.

As part of the project to build the Jerusalem Temple, David perfectly illustrated the heart of the Father. Knowing what Solomon would need to do this great work, he put all his efforts into preparing everything. Having received from Yahweh all the models and even the organization of priestly classes, he recorded everything and handed it over to Solomon. He also gave gold, silver, and all sorts of materials (1 Chronicles 28 verses 19 and 21; 1 Chronicles 29 verse 2).

Whoever understands that God is his Father will never be afraid of anything again. He is the eternal God who preceded us. He has just come back from eternity to show us the way to success. There is a plan from our Father that failure is impossible.

Although he has planned our success, he cannot impose his ways on us. Thus, predestination, according to the Scriptures, leaves great freedom to man, who constantly enjoys free will. God implements His plan when we embrace Him and decide to walk in obedience from start to finish.

Marked with the seal of the Holy Spirit

> **Ephesians 1 verse 13; KJV**
>
> In whom ye also trusted, after that ye heard the word of truth, the gospel of your salvation: in whom also after that ye believed, ye were sealed with that holy Spirit of promise,

Seal: sphragizó—affix a mark that certifies ownership with a knight or other stamping instrument (a roller or a seal).

The Holy Spirit places on whoever the Lord chooses a mark that proclaims to everyone that this person is the property of God. This is why the Holy Spirit descended on Jesus the day he was immersed in the waters. He will proclaim this fact in every city where he passes (Luke 4 verse 18).

It is for the same reason that the Holy Spirit descended on the disciples at the beginning of the Church. And let it come down on everyone who believes.

He calls all men because they were all created for his glory. Those who respond to his call are anointed (chosen). It follows that the Holy Spirit comes to put the mark of the Lord on these people. In fact, he comes upon them to enable them to fulfill their mandate.

Whoever believes does not have to beg for immersion in the

Holy Spirit and the glorious presence of God. He is loved by God. He is a son. It is dignified.

To desire God's profound things with all your heart is not to beg. It is a question of expressing our thirst to walk in the dimension of God rather than continuing to rely on natural means. The thirst to see the glory of God will still be the dividing line between those who enter and those who remain outside (John 7, verses 37 to 39).

Jews and Gentiles united in one new man

Ephesians 2 verse 15; KJV

Having abolished in his flesh the enmity, *even* the law of commandments *contained* in ordinances; for to make in himself of twain one new man, *so* making peace;

On one side, there were Jews accustomed to the law of Moses and pagans on the other—the latter followed a host of gods. Of these two groups, Jesus made one people, one family. There is in fact one Church, one immersion, one Holy Spirit, and one God (Ephesians 4 verses 4 to 6).

Jewish Christians envisioned a two-tier church: those who would continue to follow the ordinances of the Law of Moses, and those who would abstain from meat sacrificed to idols and from fornication. The Holy Spirit will bring a correction through the revelations given to Paul. Whoever is in Christ is a New Creation—he walks according to the law of Christ.

The preaching of the cross highlights the fact that we enter the kingdom of grace from the moment we recognize that Jesus has taken our place on the cross. Just as death and sin reigned over all because of Adam's single act of disobedience, God's grace and justice automatically rule over those who are in Jesus.

Romans 5 verses 17 to 18; KJV

17 For if by one man's offence death reigned by one; much more they which receive abundance of grace and of the gift of righteousness shall reign in life by one, Jesus Christ.) 18 Therefore as by the offence of one judgment came upon all men to condemnation; even so by the righteousness of one the free gift came upon all men unto justification of life.

We should stick to Jesus Christ, not to human traditions and commandments. Let us guard carefully against the religion and doctrines of men who blind and enslave those who follow them.

Colossians 2 verses 16 to 19; KJV

16 Let no man therefore judge you in meat, or in drink, or in respect of an holyday, or of the new moon, or of the sabbath days: 17 Which are a shadow of things to come; but the body is of Christ. 18 Let no man beguile you of your reward in a voluntary humility and worshipping of angels, intruding into those things which he hath not seen, vainly puffed up by his fleshly mind, 19 And not holding the Head, from which all the body by joints and bands having nourishment ministered, and knit together, increaseth with the increase of God.

A holy temple in the Lord

Ephesians 2 verse 21; KJV

In whom all the building fitly framed together groweth unto an holy temple in the Lord:

Jesus is the main stone and the foundation that the builders rejected. It is the cornerstone that gives other stones their place and direction. Those who align themselves with Him will find themselves in coordination with others.

The Church that he is building is rising through the power of his Spirit. It is not a human work. As the body of Christ, the Church is also a dwelling place of God, a holy temple.

Are we in the place he indicated? Are we moving in the right direction? What can we say about the coordination with the rest of the body?

The root cause of the lack of growth can also be found in the lack of alignment with Jesus. In Him, the well-coordinated edifice rises. There is no stagnation in our God. It is a continuous movement of the Holy Spirit.

A dwelling of God in Spirit

Ephesians 2 verse 22; KJV

In whom ye also are builded together for an habitation of God through the Spirit.

In the past, Yahweh put his presence in the tabernacle of Moses.

With Jesus and the miracle of the new birth, He can come to dwell in us by His Spirit. The incredible privilege of the new creation is that of being able to carry in our spirit the God who created everything. We are individually a dwelling place of God in Spirit. It is God's dream to show His glory through each of His children.

You must agree to be configured according to the model that comes down from the sky. Self-will, religion, and human traditions must capitulate to the infinitely great glory of our God. He is the ONLY Lord.

We do not yet have a full understanding of what it means to be a dwelling place of God in Spirit. And yet, it means what it means. The Christian is a giver of God's presence. All of God that dwells in him must be able to manifest itself as fully as it did when Jesus was walking on earth.

What can we do to possess the nature of God that he has given us as an inheritance? What can we do to overcome the limitations that old nature has placed us in? Is it possible to be fully conformed to Christ in our soul?

By submitting ourselves to the requirements of the school of the counting and consecration of the Holy Spirit, yes, it is possible to reflect Christ perfectly.

John G. Lake talks about the concept of Christ-man to express the idea of total union with Jesus.

..., but the secret of Christianity is not in doing. The secret is in being. It is to be a possessor of the nature of Jesus Christ. In other words, it is to be Christ in character, Christ in demonstration, and Christ in the transmitting agency. When a person gives himself to the Lord and becomes a child of God, a Christian, he is a Christ-Man. Everything he does and says from then on should be the will and the words and deeds of Jesus, as absolutely, and fully as Jesus spoke and did the will of the Father.

Free access to God

Ephesians 3 verse 12; KJV

In whom we have boldness and access with confidence by the faith of him.

It was the sole privilege of the priests to approach God as part of their service. Except for the high priest, who entered the most holy place once a year, the holy place was the farthest they could go. Those who were not priests stayed in the outer court, where the victims were sacrificed.

If they saw his glory in the form of a pillar of cloud during the day and in the form of a pillar of fire above the tabernacle, they were not allowed to approach under pain of death. Even priests could be put to death if they did not follow the ordinances prescribed for approaching God.

The veil that separated the holy place from the most holy place is torn from top to bottom as Jesus returns the spirit at Golgotha.

Matthew 27 verses 50 to 51; KJV

50 Jesus, when he had cried again with a loud voice, yielded up the ghost. 51 And, behold, the veil of the temple was rent in twain from the top to the bottom; and the earth did quake, and the rocks rent;

Jesus is the Way to the Father. Whoever enters through Him approaches the throne in the position of a son of God. He is clothed in the righteousness of Jesus. The Father sees Jesus in this person. He remembers the transaction of the cross. The blood of Jesus placed before Him on the mercy seat in heaven speaks for us.

Exercising faith is important. We put our trust in Jesus, who assures us that the prayers addressed to the Father in his name will be answered.

John 16 verse 23; KJV

And in that day ye shall ask me nothing. Verily, verily, I say unto you, Whatsoever ye shall ask the Father in my name, he will give it you.

Why do people lack the confidence to approach God?

It is essentially the conscience of sin that handicaps man. He said to himself, I am not good enough; I am only a poor fisherman; certainly God will not listen to me. He has his eyes set on its merits.

Within the framework set by God, we receive the justice that Jesus imparts. We are approaching the throne of grace in the name of Jesus. We approach as its representatives on earth. We received a power of attorney to speak on his behalf and for his interests. So we should no longer look at ourselves. Because it's not primarily about us, but of Him.

Ignorance of God's love greatly limits anyone who wants to approach God. If we knew what kind of love God loves us with, we would approach Him with great confidence. He loves us unconditionally. What we do does not affect the love he has for us. Can a mother forget the child she breastfed? Can a father reject someone who has, in some way, come out of his kidneys?

Let's talk like this to Israel, who was complaining about being rejected by Yahweh, He was reassuring them of his eternal love.

Isaiah 49 verses 14 to 16; KJV

14 But Zion said, The LORD hath forsaken me, and my Lord hath forgotten me. 15 Can a woman forget her sucking child, that she should not have compassion on the son of her womb? yea, they may forget, yet will I not forget thee. 16 Behold, I have graven thee upon the palms of my hands; thy walls are continually before me.

When we were children of the revolt, they already loved us 100% and he gave Jesus Christ to make us his children. Now that we are from his house and have his life in us, how would he love us less? Let's reject the lies of the devil, our Father still loves us 100%. When we fall, it shows us the blood. It is our responsibility to apply blood to be restored into full communion with Him.

1 John 1 verses 6 to 7; KJV

6 If we say that we have fellowship with him, and walk in darkness, we lie, and do not the truth: 7 But if we walk in the light, as he is in the light, we have fellowship one with another, and the blood of Jesus

Christ his Son cleanseth us from all sin.

When one approaches with confidence through faith in Jesus, one also knows that one has asked for the thing. Thus, faith does not put the thing into the future since one already has the thing requested. Faith enjoys giving thanks during the time of transfer from there to here. Glory to God.

Rooted and grounded

Colossians 2 verse 7; KJV

Rooted and built up in him, and established in the faith, as ye have been taught, abounding therein with thanksgiving.

Jesus Christ is the Rock of the Ages upon which the house of God, which is the Church, was built. It is the solid foundation that ensures the sustainability of the work.

The Lord plants and strengthens by using His Word – it is in it that power is found. He sends his word. He teaches us his ways. Whoever opens his heart and receives it through faith shows the fruit that corresponds to the seed received.

If the Christian was a tree, then God planted it in Jesus. It is in Him that our roots have been placed. So it is from Him that everything we need comes to us. He is our Source. If we knew who Jesus is, would we be limited?

He said to the Samaritan woman: *If thou knewest the gift of God, and who it is that saith to thee, Give me to drink; thou wouldest have asked of him, and he would have given thee living water. (John 4:10; KJV).*

Israel, walking in the desert, did not understand that Jesus was the Rock that walked with them to water them when they were thirsty. He was there, though, they didn't know. They kept complaining.

If we can understand that the mercy of God who planted us in Jesus has put us in the perfect place, in the place where everything we need is, we would be constantly praising.

How can we miss when we are rooted in Jehovah Jireh[1] ? Let us recognize his mercy and praise him. Our eyes see more clearly when we rent it. Closed doors also open when pure faith is shown.

---

[1] "Jehovah Jireh" is a Hebrew phrase that means "The Lord Will Provide" or "The Lord Will See to It." It comes from **Genesis 22:14** "And Abraham called the name of that place Jehovahjireh: as it is said *to* this day, In the mount of the LORD it shall be seen."

Complete, filled to capacity

> **Colossians 2 verses 9-10; KJV**
>
> 9 For in him dwelleth all the fulness of the Godhead bodily. 10 And ye are complete in him, which is the head of all principality and power

The Greek term means to be fulfilled to the fullest individual capacity. There is also the idea of being brought to its full realization.

There is nothing lacking in the one that the Father has chosen and placed in Jesus. Since ALL of God is fully manifested in Jesus, the life of each of his disciples is complete in Him. Where we see imperfections and shortcomings, the Father sees only Jesus. If we could believe that from the perspective of God, who invites us to enter into his rest that we already have, we would change the way we pray and even look at life.

Our Father is Yahweh-Shalom, the Eternal, our Peace (Shalom). In Hebrew, Shalom is the situation in which all the parties are brought together and brought to their place; none is absent. It is about the integrity of our being that we are talking about. Everything has its place in our mind, soul, and body.

Any testimony contrary to that of the Spirit of God should be ignored. This is what Jesus teaches us. As a matter of fact, He never recognized any authority to situations that were contrary to what the Father had done.

The Father knows that he placed our diseases and disabilities on Jesus. We have been delivered; we have been healed; we have overcome sin (the body of the sins of the flesh has been put off). A new heart has been given to us (Colossians 2:11).

Stripped of the body of the flesh

Colossians 2 verse 11; KJV

In whom also ye are circumcised with the circumcision made without hands, in putting off the body of the sins of the flesh by the circumcision of Christ:

The Lord had given the ordinance of circumcising Abraham and his male descendants as a sign of the perpetual covenant that bound them.

Genesis 17 verses 9-11; KJV

9 And God said unto Abraham, Thou shalt keep my covenant therefore, thou, and thy seed after thee in their generations. 10 This is my covenant, which ye shall keep, between me and you and thy seed after thee; Every man child among you shall be circumcised. 11 And ye shall circumcise the flesh of your foreskin; and it shall be a token of the covenant betwixt me and you.

He had prophetically committed this act without always under-standing its significance. On the eighth day after the birth of a boy, he was separated from the foreskin, which was cut off and carried away from him. By giving them the law and ordinances in the desert, he also promised to circumcise their hearts so that he would love and serve them.

Deuteronomy 30 verse 6 KJV

And the LORD thy God will circumcise thine heart, and the heart of thy seed, to love the LORD thy God with all thine heart, and with all thy soul, that thou mayest live.

Also in connection with this glorious promise, the day of the Great Atonement (10th day of the 7th month), following the

Atonement Sacrifice, the goat was brought near to Azazel, and the high priest placed his two hands on his head and confessed Israel's iniquities and transgressions upon him. The goat was driven out of the camp into a deserted land. It removed iniquity and sin.

Leviticus 16 verses 20-22; KJV

20 And when he hath made an end of reconciling the holy place, and the tabernacle of the congregation, and the altar, he shall bring the live goat: 21 And Aaron shall lay both his hands upon the head of the live goat, and confess over him all the iniquities of the children of Israel, and all their transgressions in all their sins, putting them upon the head of the goat, and shall send him away by the hand of a fit man into the wilderness: 22 And the goat shall bear upon him all their iniquities unto a land not inhabited: and he shall let go the goat in the wilderness.

It was in Jesus Christ, who died outside the city, that the power of sin was broken. He has brought away from us the iniquity that made us unable to produce the fruits of justice.

On the cross, the Father laid our iniquities and transgressions upon Him. His death is legally the death of all who believe. His resurrection is also their resurrection. God removed the heart of stone in order to replace it with a heart of flesh. The nature of the devil, which is iniquity, has been removed—all things have become new. It is the nature of God that is there.

Abraham saw the days of Christ and rejoiced.

John 8 verse 56; KJV

Your father Abraham rejoiced to see my day: and he saw *it*, and was glad.

The circumcision order and the goat being chased out of the camp were for a while. The reality of separation from iniquity is fulfilled in Jesus Christ.

In these last times, the children of Abraham are those who are circumcised in heart. Circumcision of the flesh served its purpose.

Romans 2 verses 28-29; KJV

28 For he is not a Jew, which is one outwardly; neither is that circumcision, which is outward in the flesh: 29 But he is a Jew, which is one inwardly; and circumcision is that of the heart, in the spirit, and not in the letter; whose praise is not of men, but of God.

Whoever is in Jesus is separated from iniquity. It is a new creation. Under the guidance of the Holy Spirit, he perfected his salvation by removing from his life the things that old nature taught him.

Romans 12 verses 1 to 2; KJV

1 I beseech you therefore, brethren, by the mercies of God, that ye present your bodies a living sacrifice, holy, acceptable unto God, which is your reasonable service. 2 And be not conformed to this world: but be ye transformed by the renewing of your mind, that ye may prove what is that good, and acceptable, and perfect, will of God.

In Christ

Blessed with all heavenly blessings

Ephesians 1 verse 3; KJV

Blessed *be* the God and Father of our Lord Jesus Christ, who hath blessed us with all spiritual blessings in heavenly *places* in Christ:

The Father did not give up on the dream of making us participants in his kingdom and glory. Since everything he has also belongs to Jesus, he recreated us in Jesus to make us Jesus' children and joint heirs.

The fullness of God and grace upon grace came freely to us through Jesus Christ (John 1 verse 16). It is to the Holy Spirit that the mission of fulfilling us has been entrusted. He is actively working to ensure that all of God's promises are fulfilled in our lives.

John 16 verses 14 to 15; KJV

14 He shall glorify me: for he shall receive of mine, and

shall shew it unto you. 15 All things that the Father hath are mine: therefore said I, that he shall take of mine, and shall shew it unto you.

In Jesus, we have everything we need. We are not missing anything. In the treasures of heaven lies the bulk of our wealth. We need to work with the Holy Spirit to bring here what we already have and what is there.

The Lord Jesus was in perfect calm no matter what situations he might find himself in because he mastered the art of transferring wealth from there to here.

When he is told that there is not enough bread to feed the crowd, he ignores this information and asks his followers to have them sit down in groups of 50. Turning to the Father, he gives thanks, and the Holy Spirit multiplies what is available.

When he is taken to Lazarus' tomb and told that he has been there for four days, he ignores this information. Relying on the Holy Spirit, he calls Lazarus from death to life.

Someone might say, But Jesus was God!!! Jesus stripped himself of his glory to walk the earth as a man filled with the Holy Spirit. That is why he said that whoever believes can do the things that he has done.

John 14 verses 12 to 14; KJV

12 Verily, verily, I say unto you, He that believeth on me, the works that I do shall he do also; and greater works than these shall he do; because I go unto my Father. 13 And whatsoever ye shall ask in my name, that will I do, that the Father may be glorified in the Son. 14 If ye shall ask any thing in my name, I will do it.

If it is true that we do not lack anything and that we can do the same works as Jesus, what could be the reasons for our weaknesses and defeats?

The Holy Spirit was already saying about Israel that they were in trouble because of their lack of knowledge of spiritual things (Hosea 4 verse 6).

Could this reason apply to modern-day Christians? What could have happened between the time of the first churches and the time we are in?

Could it be that we have abandoned the things that Jesus prescribed to the apostles? A careful reading of the scriptures seems to reveal that this is the case. We are being defeated because we lack knowledge.

The Holy Spirit wants to reveal to us things we don't know. The blockages are not the work of God, who has already given.

Jeremiah 33 verse 3; KJV

Call unto me, and I will answer thee, and shew thee great and mighty things, which thou knowest not.

Prayer: Father, in the name of Jesus, you have said that darkness will not always reign; let me know great things, hidden things that I do not yet know—those that are for my complete deliverance and those that are for my elevation in Jesus and my establishment as the son of God.

United with the things that are in heaven

Ephesians 1 verse 10; KJV

That in the dispensation of the fullness of times he might gather together in one all things in Christ, both which are in heaven, and which are on earth; even in him:

In the past, we were strangers to the life of God. In Him, we became participants in the life of God. The Church of Jesus in general and Christians in particular are extensions of heaven on earth. God is our Father; Jesus is our big brother, and angels are our fellow servants. We are vibrating at the frequency of the Heaven.

Our resources are endless because we are in communion with the Father and the Son through the Holy Spirit. Our domain is the home of our God, who is above all heaven.

Let's ignore the limitations that are right in front of our natural eyes. United with Jesus, we are fulfilled. We don't lack anything.

So let praise be on our lips constantly. Because he did great things for us.

Forgiven, and forgiving

Ephesians 4 verse 32; KJV

And be ye kind one to another, tenderhearted, forgiving one another, even as God for Christ's sake hath forgiven you.

Overcome with guilt and shame after his fall, Adam was hiding from God. Satan is the one who seduces and leads to sin. He is also the one who takes pleasure in tormenting the one who has fallen. The wages of sin is death. Whoever sins will fall under the dominion of the destroyer. Being in the chains of death and sin, he can neither have peace nor enter into the fullness of his inheritance.

God's mercy offers forgiveness—which is the power that frees the captive from shackles. As long as the human heart is trapped in guilt, it is unable to receive what the Father gives. This is why Jesus said to the disabled person who had been carried away by his friends and laid before the Lord: your sins are forgiven you.

Luke 5 verses 19 to 26; KJV

19 And when they could not find by what way they might bring him in because of the multitude, they went upon the housetop, and let him down through

the tiling with his couch into the midst before Jesus. 20 And when he saw their faith, he said unto him, Man, thy sins are forgiven thee. 21 And the scribes and the Pharisees began to reason, saying, Who is this which speaketh blasphemies? Who can forgive sins, but God alone? 22 But when Jesus perceived their thoughts, he answering said unto them, What reason ye in your hearts? 23 Whether is easier, to say, Thy sins be forgiven thee; or to say, Rise up and walk? 24 But that ye may know that the Son of man hath power upon earth to forgive sins, (he said unto the sick of the palsy,) I say unto thee, Arise, and take up thy couch, and go into thine house. 25 And immediately he rose up before them, and took up that whereon he lay, and departed to his own house, glorifying God. 26 And they were all amazed, and they glorified God, and were filled with fear, saying, We have seen strange things to day.

Many people find themselves unable to accept what God provides because their hearts are burdened with feelings of guilt, resentment, or other similar emotions.

In Jesus, the Father forgave us. Healing and deliverance will come quickly to those who open their hearts to the work of the Holy Spirit. It speaks of repentance—one must turn away from iniquity and sin.

When I forgive the person who offended me, the legal basis on which the torturers stood to torment me is destroyed. We will still be measured with the same measure we used to measure others.

To forgive the person who has offended us is to do our first service.

When I bless my enemy or whoever has offended me, I am the first to benefit from the flow of grace that comes through my heart and mouth before it is poured out on him. Let us develop the habit of praying for those who persecute us and of blessing our enemies.

Matthew 5 verse 43-48; KJV

43 Ye have heard that it hath been said, Thou shalt love thy neighbour, and hate thine enemy. 44 But I say unto you, Love your enemies, bless them that curse you, do good to them that hate you, and pray for them which despitefully use you, and persecute you; 45 That ye may be the children of your Father which is in heaven: for he maketh his sun to rise on the evil and on the good, and sendeth rain on the just and on the unjust. 46 For if ye love them which love you, what reward have ye? do not even the publicans the same? 47 And if ye salute your brethren only, what do ye more than others? do not even the publicans so? 48 Be ye therefore perfect, even as your Father which

is in heaven is perfect.

No one can condemn the person whom the Father has freed. Let us not allow the lies and insinuations of the devil to take root in our thoughts.

Immersed in the waters: put on Christ

Galatians 3 verse 27; KJV

For as many of you as have been baptized into Christ have put on Christ.

Through faith, we are children of God, because those who have received us have been recreated by the power of the Holy Spirit. By immersing us in water in His name, the Father placed us in Him. The Greek term translated "put on" literally means that we have slipped into Jesus, much like we slip into a garment. In an instant, what was not there before became ours. Everything he is, everything he owns, has been transferred to us.

Let us resist the temptation to think of ourselves as humans since what was is no longer there—a new, dominant reality is here. The life of Christ that is within us is called to take full place in our spirit as well as in our soul and body.

It is up to us to make use of the resources and means that the Father has put at our disposal. It is obvious that if we do not know what we have or who we are, we will tend to do what we have always done.

The kingdom of God is for violent people. The one who works to dismantle everything that is part of the old system and who strives to walk in the light of what reveals the Holy Spirit will gradually be established in the dimension of the Sons of God.

It is one thing to be a child of God, it is quite another to walk in the dimension of sons. May we set our sights on the goal and sacrifice everything that is necessary to achieve it. The one Who is our Father also preceded us. His glory lies in the execution of the plans he has prepared for each of his children.

Let us think like our Lord. Let's talk and act like Him. Let us publish his decrees on earth. Let us not give up on the things that he has given us. He is in us to lead us to the end. He will welcome us in glory when we complete our assignment.

By Him

Created for Him

Colossians 1 verse 16; KJV

For by him were all things created, that are in heaven, and that are in earth, visible and invisible, whether *they be* thrones, or dominions, or principalities, or powers: all things were created by him, and for him:

Understanding that neither worlds nor humans emerge from nothing, contrary to what some may suggest, but rather everything is created by God for His glory and our benefit, provides us with a firm foundation for building our lives.

The earth and everything in it belong to Jesus. He is particularly concerned about the life of each person. He cares about our well-being because he is the one who decided to bring us into this world.

As the first manager, he planned everything. But he can't force anything on us. The one who opens his heart to him and says "Yes" to his plans will see the Spirit of God guide him on the path of achievement so desired by all men.

What is unfortunately unknown to the majority is that achievement is impossible by the sole will of man, who is otherwise confused and dominated by iniquity.

Reconciled with God

Colossians 1 verse 20; KJV

And, having made peace through the blood of his cross, by him to reconcile all things unto himself; by him, *I say*, whether *they be* things in earth, or things in heaven.

God visited the earth in the person of Jesus Christ in order to bring man back into the position of sons of God. He became a man to acquire the right to pay the price of our rebellion on our behalf.

Separated from God, the natural man, no matter what he thinks or says, is under the ferocious domination of the devil (1 John 5 verse 19). The egocentrism and pride that are in each of us show more than enough that we have a nasty problem. Created in the image of God, man assumed the nature of the devil when he submitted to him.

Those who put their trust in the redemptive work of the cross pass from death to life. God has set a day when he will remove evil from creation. Jesus is the One through whom everything that is in heaven and what is on earth will once again unite in perfect harmony.

Whoever is in Jesus is already experiencing this harmony—the power and glory of the world to come are present in the life of a follower of Jesus. The Holy Spirit, who has administered the Church since the day of Pentecost, will ensure that we know the things of God.

Access to God

Ephesians 2 verse 18; KJV

For through him we both have access by one Spirit unto the Father.

From the very beginning, he showed Adam and his sons how to worship God, how to invoke him. Abel's offering shows that he understood the mystery of the altars. Whoever owns the altar will show his presence if the indicated protocol is followed.

Exodus 20 verses 24-26; KJV

24 An altar of earth thou shalt make unto me, and shalt sacrifice thereon thy burnt offerings, and thy peace offerings, thy sheep, and thine oxen: in all places where I record my name I will come unto thee, and I will bless thee. 25 And if thou wilt make me an altar of stone, thou shalt not build it of hewn stone: for if thou lift up thy tool upon it, thou hast polluted it. 26 Neither shalt thou go up by steps unto mine altar, that thy nakedness be not discovered thereon.

The offerings remind us of the person to whom the altar belongs, the covenant made, and his promises. Yahweh remembered that his name had been placed on the altar. He was forced to come to the worshiper to bless him.

The Lord put the things to offer into their hands (Exodus 10:25). It also gave the laws and protocols to follow to open the doors of blessings. He gave Jesus, the Lamb of God, the perfect sacrifice that gives us access to all the wealth of heaven.

Nobody went to the holy place or to the Holy of Holies without first going through the Altar of Sacrifice. Passing through the cross is necessary for anyone who wants to live by the Spirit and who wants to enter the place where God shows his glory.

You have to die to be reborn and to live fully. When the altar was made of stone, it was not made of cut stones. The chisel on the stone desecrates the altar. Human work is excluded from what God does. It is God who is at work from start to finish. We die to ourselves, to our principles and values, to adopt hers.

Many people struggle with the Holy Spirit. They would like to get the right to move on with the things that belong to this world. He who gave the Lamb that comes from heaven and the ordinances that come from heaven was also the one who said not to build an altar with stones trimmed. He will not accept things that come from man. Let us allow ourselves to be stripped of the things that limit us.

Many would like to invent another path; they would like to propose another model. God will not accept models that come from men. The scriptures abound with tragic tales that must resonate with us :

The tragic deaths of Aaron's sons

Leviticus 10 verses 1 to 3; KJV

1 And Nadab and Abihu, the sons of Aaron, took either of them his censer, and put fire therein, and put incense thereon, and offered strange fire before the LORD, which he commanded them not. 2 And there went out fire from the LORD, and devoured them, and

they died before the LORD. 3 Then Moses said unto Aaron, This is it that the LORD spake, saying, I will be sanctified in them that come nigh me, and before all the people I will be glorified. And Aaron held his peace.

The death of Uzza during the first attempt to carry the tabernacle to Jerusalem

1 Chronicles 13 verses 9-10; KJV

9 And when they came unto the threshing floor of Chidon, Uzza put forth his hand to hold the ark; for the oxen stumbled. 10 And the anger of the LORD was kindled against Uzza, and he smote him, because he put his hand to the ark: and there he died before God.

1 Chronicles 15 verses 1 to 2; KJV

1 And David made him houses in the city of David, and prepared a place for the ark of God, and pitched for it a tent. 2 Then David said, None ought to carry the ark of God but the Levites: for them hath the LORD chosen to carry the ark of God, and to minister unto him forever.

We are in communion with the Father and the Son through the Holy Spirit. Note that the scriptures do not talk about other intermediaries.

We pray to the Father in the name of Jesus Christ. Let us beware of offering the side to the destroyer. Let us guard against idolatry . Let us stick to what the Lord has prescribed for the Church.

Traditions that don't follow the pattern that comes down from heaven should be recognized as altars to be demolished. There will be no peace in the life of anyone who keeps them active in their life. Because He[2] who inspired them, will come again to steal, destroy, and kill.

Let us meditate again on these words:

1 Timothy 2 verse 5; KJV

That your faith should not stand in the wisdom of men, but in the power of God.

Acts 4 verse 12; KJV

Neither is there salvation in any other: for there is

---

[2] He stands here for the Devil, who seeks ways to the plans of God in our lives.

none other name under heaven given among men, whereby we must be saved.

Revelation 22 verses 18 to 19; KJV

18 For I testify unto every man that heareth the words of the prophecy of this book, If any man shall add unto these things, God shall add unto him the plagues that are written in this book: 19 And if any man shall take away from the words of the book of this prophecy, God shall take away his part out of the book of life, and out of the holy city, and from the things which are written in this book.

Purified and zealous for good works

Title 2, verse 14; KJV

Who gave himself for us, that he might redeem us from all iniquity, and purify unto himself a peculiar people, zealous of good works.

Having seen our misery and poverty, Jesus came down from heaven to go to the cross in our place. He took charge of our iniquity and transgressions. He paid our debt to become the owner of our lives.

Since he has purified us, there is no longer any legal basis for conviction. Curses, enchantments, spells—any weapon trained against us will not thrive. In fact, no one can condemn God's chosen people.

Let us methodically apply blood to our lives and those of our loved ones to fully benefit from what happened at Golgotha. Individual denunciation of iniquities and transgressions is important to establish and seal the freedom of those who groaned in the dungeons of the devil.

Established in the office of priest

Hebrews 13 verse 15; KJV

By him therefore let us offer the sacrifice of praise to God continually, that is, the fruit of *our* lips giving thanks to his name.

The privilege of approaching God to offer sacrifices was reserved only to priests. Once a year, the high priest went into the most holy place to deposit the blood of the atonement on the mercy seat.

In Jesus, God created a nation of priest-kings; all have the privilege of coming into his presence to worship and celebrate him. The sacrifice that we offer by Jesus is the fruit of our lips that confess his name.

1 Peter 2 verses 9-10; KJV

9 But ye are a chosen generation, a royal priesthood, an holy nation, a peculiar people; that ye should shew forth the praises of him who hath called you out of darkness into his marvellous light: 10 Which in time past were not a people, but are now the people of God: which had not obtained mercy, but now have obtained mercy.

Whoever wants to honor God must submit to the order that he has put forth. Every man must submit to Jesus, who is the One to whom all power in heaven and on earth has been handed over.

The revelation of God and communion with him pass through

Jesus. Those who abide in Jesus enjoy an infinitely great privilege. The Holy Spirit gives him everything that is Jesus' and he can enter into the glory of the One who dwells in a light inaccessible to ordinary mortals.

Rescued from the wrath of God

Romans 5 verse 9; KJV

Much more then, being now justified by his blood, we shall be saved from wrath through him.

Romans 5 verse 17; KJV

For if by one man's offense death reigned by one; much more they which receive abundance of grace and of the gift of righteousness shall reign in life by one, Jesus Christ.)

Everything we are, everything we have, and everything we are capable of doing is found in Jesus Christ. It is through Him that we rule.

He gave the Church the power to bind and unbind. Through the delegation of power that he has given us, we act as his representatives on earth. The Spirit of God is given by virtue of what he did at the cross. Angels obey the voice of His Word that we proclaim by virtue of the right of representation that we have.

In his name, demons flee because they recognize the authority with which we are vested. The power is in his name.

The key to glory lies in our ability to abide in Him, where the abundance of grace and the gift of justice reside. The active power of God is fully available in Jesus, who is also our justice.

As automatically as the rebellious nature of the devil ruled over us through Adam, the nature of God, which is justice, is destined to rule over those who are descended from Jesus.

No effort was needed to participate in the inequity. Naturally, the rebel produces works of injustice; in the same way, no effort is needed to produce works of justice when one understands the parallelism of form presented by the Holy Spirit.

We are limited by what we believe. The words of Yahweh truly resonate when sons continue to think and behave as though they are slaves:

Psalm 82 verses 6 to 7; KJV

6 I have said, Ye are gods; and all of you are children of the most High. 7 But ye shall die like men, and fall like one of the princes.

It is not in the physical realms that we should seek proof of the great work that the Father has done in us through his Spirit. Let us abstain from knowing the one who is in Christ in a natural way. Even the glorified Jesus is completely different from the one who walked the earth.

2 Corinthians 5 verse 16; KJV

Wherefore henceforth know we no man after the flesh: yea, though we have known Christ after the flesh, yet now henceforth know we him no more.

Let us believe in the testimony of the Holy Spirit about those who have passed through the cross. Whoever is in Jesus is a New Creation. That which is human has been. God dwells in him through his Spirit.

2 Corinthians 5 verse 17; KJV

Therefore if any man *be* in Christ, *he is* a new creature: old things are passed away; behold, all things are become new.

It is through faith that we enter into the dimension of God. It is also through faith that we maintain ourselves there. Whoever gives glory to the Father and who persists in acting as a son of God will see himself established in him the things of heaven.

With him

The same plant in its death and in its resurrection

Romans 6 verses 4 to 5; KJV

4 Therefore we are buried with him by baptism into death: that like as Christ was raised up from the dead by the glory of the Father, even so we also should walk in newness of life. 5 For if we have been planted together in the likeness of his death, we shall be also in the likeness of his resurrection:

The path to glory begins with death. The brazen Altar[3] was the first thing you came to when you entered the door of Moses' Tabernacle. It is the place where the worshiper laid hands on the victim to confess his iniquities and sins before the victim was put to death in his place. It is the symbol of the cross, where the natural man is put to death.

Since man was created in the image of God, the blood of goats could not take away his iniquities and sins. Thus, it was necessary for God Himself to come in the person of Jesus to redeem the one who had been created in his image.

The Father unites to Jesus at the cross anyone who confesses that he is his representative. It is on Jesus that we lay our sins. Since he is dead, we are dead. He paid our debt; we are out of debt.

Having gone down to hell, he spent three nights and three days atoning for our sins. When God's justice was fully satisfied, he brought him back from death to life. His resurrection and return to glory are our resurrection and our return to glory.

When the work of the Cross has become complete in a man's life, the life of the Risen One is naturally his life. There is no effort to make. He will take all the space that we dedicate to Him. It is through death to ourselves that we dedicate our whole being to Him.

---

[3] The brazen altar was made with bronze. It was on it that sacrifices were offered.

That is why the Holy Spirit will lead us again on the path of renunciation and consecration. The natural man (the outside man) must be completely destroyed in order for the glory that is hidden within to appear.

No more slaves to sin

Romans 6 verse 6; NKJV

Knowing this, that our old man is crucified with him, that the body of sin might be destroyed, that henceforth we should not serve sin.

We have authority over the devil, over iniquity, over sin, and over disease—he has freed us from all the limitations of the past. When temptation comes, let us remember that we have defeated the devil. Let us draw on the life of God that is within us. We don't lack anything.

Sin is the property of the devil. He will find a way to limit or destroy us if we disregard the anointing we have received. The glorious call that the Father has given us is to walk like children of God.

Satan will want to drag us into the field of compromise. He has a better understanding of spiritual things than the majority of Christians. It is not true that compromise is the only option.

If loved ones turn their backs on us because of our commitment to justice, let's be happy with what we've shown our fidelity to Jesus. For Him, obedience is proof of love.

United in death and in life

> **Romans 6 verse 8; KJV**
>
> Now if we be dead with Christ, we believe that we shall also live with him

The one who took charge of our iniquity and our sin, and who died in our place, was brought back from death to life.

> **Revelation 1 verses 17 to 18; KJV**
>
> 17 And when I saw him, I fell at his feet as dead. And he laid his right hand upon me, saying unto me, Fear

> not; I am the first and the last: 18 I am he that liveth,
> and was dead; and, behold, I am alive for evermore,
> Amen; and have the keys of hell and of death.

Since he has conquered death and holds the keys to death and Hades, how can they dominate or restrain us?

Whoever believes in Jesus will live even though his body is dead. Moreover, a day has been set when he will give heavenly bodies to his followers—the resurrection of the dead is the great hope of Christians. We will live with Him with our spirit, soul, and body. The three dimensions of our being will have experienced all the dimensions of the great salvation that is in Jesus.

In the meantime, the resurrection of the bodies, we can already walk in the power of resurrection. Aware of our union with Him, we can be established in the righteousness of God and the glory of God to walk as He walked in this world.

The death of Jesus is credited to us in exactly the same way. so that his justice is brought to our credit. In the redemptive work, Jesus was our representative from start to finish.

It is important to remember that what is imputed (legally attributed) must be established through a systematic process of renunciation, brokenness, and consecration. Understanding what he did for us, we decided to turn our back on our old ways of thinking and acting.

> **2 Corinthians 5 verses 14 to 15; KJV**
>
> 14 For the love of Christ constraineth us; because we thus judge, that if one died for all, then were all dead: 15 And that he died for all, that they which live should not henceforth live unto themselves, but unto him which died for them, and rose again.

Whoever humbles himself under the power of God, and chooses to be docile and have good will to always go where the Spirit of God leads is engaged in a process of death—the destruction of iniquity.

At the same time, a life process is underway in him. The Word of God establishes him in the righteousness of God and in the glory of God.

It is necessary to die to what is carnal to live in the dimension of God. This is the glorious call of our Father for every man. Note that there is a price to pay. Are you ready to pay the consecration price that the Holy Spirit may require for the power you would like to demonstrate?

United in His glory at the end of all things

Colossians 3 verse 4; KJV

When Christ, who is our life, shall appear, then shall ye also appear with him in glory.

Through the miracle of the new birth, the Father recreates the person who trusts in the work of the cross in Jesus. At the school of the stripping and consecration of the Holy Spirit, the new disciple is led in the process of transforming his soul.

The aim is for Jesus to be perfectly formed in us. It has to be our life. As the disciple grows in understanding of his unity with the Master, he increasingly perceives and articulates the thoughts and deeds of the One residing within him. This is the consequence of the awareness of union with Jesus (1 Corinthians 6 verse 17).

Whoever is docile and obedient will gradually be established in the justice and glory of God. He will walk the earth in a significant measure of authority.

If we will appear with Him in His glory at the end of all things, He should be able to appear with us today as we represent Him on earth.

We know that we gave up on ourselves when we stopped resisting the Holy Spirit. Many people ignore the simple instructions of the Scriptures; they think they are subject to private interpretation—as if the Lord expected men to do as they see fit.

The truth is that he has clearly stated his thinking. It is dark to anyone who rejects the Spirit of God and the simplicity of the gospel of Christ. Light comes easily when you recognize that Jesus is the Light and decide to follow Him.

We know he is our life when we stick to what he said and did. If we cannot find strong support in the scriptures for the practices we have inherited from those who taught us Christ, let us reject them.

1 Corinthians 11 verse 1; KJV

Be ye followers of me, even as I also *am* of Christ.

The principle stated here is this: no one has the right to follow a person who claims to speak in the name of Jesus and who does not follow him.

How do you know if a person is not following Jesus? It's very simple: it will twist the scriptures. It will subtract and/or add.

The Holy Spirit gives us the Bereans as an example: they looked up the Scriptures to find out if what Paul said to them was true. They were looking at the 39 books of the Old Testament (The Law and the Prophets) - that was the Word of God at the time.

It was with the apostle John in the years 90-95 that the last book of the Bible was written. It ends with a clear warning:

Revelation 22 verses 18 to 19; KJV

18 For I testify unto every man that heareth the words of the prophecy of this book, If any man shall add unto these things, God shall add unto him the plagues that are written in this book: 19 And if any man shall take away from the words of the book of this prophecy, God shall take away his part out of the book of life, and out of the holy city, and from the things which are written in this book.

Those who have ears to hear what the Holy Spirit says will not understand that nothing written after the revelation of Jesus to John can replace what was said in the 66 books given to the Church.

One Spirit with the Lord

1 Corinthians 6 verse 17; KJV

But he that is joined unto the Lord is one spirit.

In the same way that whoever attaches himself to a woman becomes one body with her, whoever attaches himself to the Lord is one spirit with Him. May we grasp the significance of this spiritual law, whose respect has great benefits. Those who choose to ignore it can pay a heavy price.

Illegitimate sexual relations are known in the spiritual world as the preferred means of destroying those who engage in them. More than organic flows, there are exchanges on a spiritual and emotional level that are taking place.

Prostitutes are warehouses for demons and, at the very least, unconscious witches. Those who go to them are fools who unwittingly go down into the valleys of hell. They will be under the control of the spirits that dwell within them.

Proverbs 9 verses 13 to 18; KJV

13 A foolish woman is clamorous: she is simple, and

knoweth nothing. 14 For she sitteth at the door of her house, on a seat in the high places of the city, 15 To call passengers who go right on their ways: 16 Whoso is simple, let him turn in hither: and as for him that wanteth understanding, she saith to him, 17 Stolen waters are sweet, and bread eaten in secret is pleasant. 18 But he knoweth not that the dead are there; and that her guests are in the depths of hell.

Jesus compares the union that binds us to Him to that which binds Him to the Father:

John 17 verses 20 to 23; KJV

20 Neither pray I for these alone, but for them also which shall believe on me through their word; 21 That they all may be one; as thou, Father, art in me, and I in thee, that they also may be one in us: that the world may believe that thou hast sent me. 22 And the glory which thou gavest me I have given them; that they may be one, even as we are one: 23 I in them, and thou in me, that they may be made perfect in one; and that the world may know that thou hast sent me, and hast loved them, as thou hast loved me.

Whoever clings to the Lord is in the Lord and the Lord is in him. In the spiritual world, it's hard to tell the difference between one and the other because there are times when they merge. They go into each other.

Our spirit is thus united with that of the Lord. Everything that is in Him is in us. Its strength is our strength. His abilities are our abilities. His wisdom is our wisdom. His holiness is our holiness.

Maturity in Jesus also means walking in the faith of what this powerful principle of Union with Jesus proclaims.

Let us therefore refrain from separating what the Father has united. He united us with Jesus. Let's stop seeing ourselves separated from Him. The dimension of sons requires that we see ourselves in everything in Him and that we do through Him, with Him, and for His glory.

It requires learning. You have to choose to believe the witness of the Holy Spirit and enter this place by faith. It is maintained by faith. The Holy Spirit will show the price of the consecration to be paid. Whoever approaches the Lord must distance himself from sin and sometimes from all that is common.

3

The normal Christian life is supernatural

Jesus is the model that comes down from heaven

The concept of the model that comes down from Heaven

Throughout scripture, a consistent pattern emerges: God creates all things through His word, manifesting the divine visions and purposes that exist within His nature. When he asks a man to do something, he gives him precise plans, detailed instructions, and all the means necessary for the realization of the project.

Noah had received detailed instructions for building the ark:

Genesis 6 verses 14 to 16; KJV

> 13 And God said unto Noah, The end of all flesh is come before me; for the earth is filled with violence through them; and, behold, I will destroy them with the earth. 14 Make thee an ark of gopher wood; rooms shalt thou make in the ark, and shalt pitch it within and without with pitch. 15 And this is the fashion which thou shalt make it of: The length of the ark shall be three hundred cubits, the breadth of it fifty cubits, and the height of it thirty cubits. 16 A window shalt thou make to the ark, and in a cubit shalt thou finish it above; and the door of the ark shalt thou set in the side thereof; with lower, second, and third stories shalt thou make it.

Twice, the Holy Spirit said that Noah did everything that the Lord had commanded him (Genesis 6:22; Genesis 7:5).

God's project would not have been a success if Noah had not submitted to the guidance of the Holy Spirit. There is a pattern that comes down from Heaven. Indeed, it is not up to man when he walks to direct his steps (Jeremiah 10 verse 23) .

The Lord had given Moses precise instructions about the Tabernacle that he was to build:

> **Exodus 25 verse 2, verses 8 and 9, verse 40; KJV**
>
> 2 Speak unto the children of Israel, that they bring

me an offering: of every man that giveth it willingly with his heart ye shall take my offering. 8 And let them make me a sanctuary; that I may dwell among them. 9 According to all that I shew thee, after the pattern of the tabernacle, and the pattern of all the instruments thereof, even so shall ye make it. 40 And look that thou make them after their pattern, which was shewed thee in the mount.

Chapters 25 to 31 describe everything that needed to be built in great detail. Betsaleel, son of Uri, son of Hur, from the tribe of Judah, is chosen by God to make inventions, to work with gold, silver, and brass, to engrave stones, to work with wood, and to execute all kinds of works. God filled him with the Spirit of God, wisdom, intelligence, and knowledge for all sorts of works (Exodus 31 verses 1 to 5).

In order to make his ways known to them and to teach them how to keep themselves holy, he will teach them the law of the holocaust, the offering, the sin sacrifice, the consecration, and the sacrifice of thanksgiving. These are described in great detail in the first seven chapters of Leviticus.

The creator who made man in His own image and likeness will guide us, ensuring that heaven's presence is felt in every aspect of our lives. So he will give the Holy Spirit to whoever he chooses. The Holy Spirit comes as Lord and Master. In the desert, he walked before them in the form of a cloud during the day and in the form of a pillar of fire during the night. Those who are led by the Spirit of God are sons of God (Romans 8:14).

David received precise instructions concerning the construction of the temple that was to serve as the home of the Tabernacle of the Lord.

1 Chronicles 28 verses 11 to 19; KJV

11 Then David gave to Solomon his son the pattern of the porch, and of the houses thereof, and of the treasuries thereof, and of the upper chambers thereof, and of the inner parlours thereof, and of the place of the mercy seat, 12 And the pattern of all that he had by the spirit, of the courts of the house of the LORD, and of all the chambers round about, of the treasuries of the house of God, and of the treasuries of the dedicated things: 13 Also for the courses of the priests and the Levites, and for all the work of the service of the house of the LORD, and for all the vessels of service in the house of the LORD. 14 He gave of gold by weight for things of gold, for all instruments of all manner of service; silver also for all instruments of silver by weight, for all instruments of every kind of service: 15 Even the weight for the candlesticks of gold, and for their lamps of gold, by weight for every candlestick, and for the lamps thereof: and for the candlesticks of silver by weight, both for the candlestick, and also for the lamps thereof, according to the use of every candlestick. 16 And by weight he

gave gold for the tables of shewbread, for every table; and likewise silver for the tables of silver: 17 Also pure gold for the fleshhooks, and the bowls, and the cups: and for the golden basons he gave gold by weight for every bason; and likewise silver by weight for every bason of silver: 18 And for the altar of incense refined gold by weight; and gold for the pattern of the chariot of the cherubims, that spread out their wings, and covered the ark of the covenant of the LORD. 19 All this, said David, the LORD made me understand in writing by his hand upon me, even all the works of this pattern.

The divine pattern extended even to administrative details, as demonstrated by the systematic organization of priests and Levites into service classes, illustrating God's comprehensive oversight of His kingdom's structure. To truly experience His glory and reign, the model we adhere to must be heavenly in origin.

The preaching of repentance is at the heart of the new covenant because God does not want to build on the foundation of men. The natural man is put to death on the cross so that the new man may live. To the one who has been made a new creation through the cross, the Spirit of God says: Do not conform to the present age but be transformed by renewing your mind to know what God's will is (Romans 12:2).

By fulfilling all of God's justice, Jesus became the head of the

New Creation. It is in Him and through Him that the abundant life of God is given. He is at the same time our Source, our Destination and also our Path. He is our Source because it is in Him that we have been recreated . He is our Destination because the Holy Spirit works to ensure that Christ is perfectly formed in us—in our soul. He is the Way, because we are following in his footsteps. Indeed, it is fitting for a disciple to emulate his master. Our eyes are fixed on Him as we make our pilgrimage on earth.

The divine paradigm revealed from heaven stands in stark contrast to human-derived commandments and traditions, which cannot produce authentic spiritual transformation. Human commandments and their traditions are the basis of religious systems. While those who follow them may be zealous, they lack knowledge. Human commandments and traditions cannot give life. It is by following the Truth (the model that comes down from heaven) that we achieve freedom.

Let us look at some important aspects of the life of Jesus that we would do well to follow as disciples.

His submission to God and the Holy Spirit

In the early hours of his ministry, Jesus proclaimed his submission to God and the Holy Spirit by declaring the prophet Isaiah's prophecy fulfilled, describing the works that the Messiah would perform.

Luke 4 verses 18 to 19; KJV

18 The Spirit of the Lord is upon me, because he hath anointed me to preach the gospel to the poor; he hath sent me to heal the brokenhearted, to preach deliverance to the captives, and recovering of sight to the blind, to set at liberty them that are bruised, 19 To preach the acceptable year of the Lord. 20 And he closed the book, and he gave it again to the minister, and sat down. And the eyes of all them that were in the synagogue were fastened on him.

Certainly, the One who chooses and sends is greater than the One who is anointed and sent. Jesus recognizes that he came from the Father, who gave him his Spirit. Submitting to the Father, who declares the end of everything from the beginning, Jesus declares the prophecy fulfilled.

He will remain constant in both his words and his actions.

John 8 verse 25-30; KJV

25 Then said they unto him, Who art thou? And Jesus saith unto them, Even the same that I said unto you from the beginning. 26 I have many things to say and to judge of you: but he that sent me is true; and I speak

to the world those things which I have heard of him. 27 They understood not that he spake to them of the Father. 28 Then said Jesus unto them, When ye have lifted up the Son of man, then shall ye know that I am he, and that I do nothing of myself; but as my Father hath taught me, I speak these things. 29 And he that sent me is with me: the Father hath not left me alone; for I do always those things that please him. 30 As he spake these words, many believed on him.

His ardent desire to destroy the works of the devil

Luke 4 verses 18 to 19; KJV

18 The Spirit of the Lord is upon me, because he hath anointed me to preach the gospel to the poor; he hath sent me to heal the brokenhearted, to preach deliverance to the captives, and recovering of sight to the blind, to set at liberty them that are bruised, 19 To preach the acceptable year of the Lord.

Jesus had looked in the book of the prophet Isaiah for the text that spoke of his ministry and read it in the presence of all those who had come to the synagogue that particular Sabbath day in

Nazareth.

He was aware that the Father had chosen him to enter this world and dismantle the devil's deeds.

Man is spiritually poor as long as he remains far from the Extraordinary Covenant that Jesus inaugurated with his blood. The greatest and most precious promises of God constitute the inheritance of those who are born of God.

Numerous individuals experience oppression from impure spirits in various aspects of their lives. They seek natural solutions to problems whose roots are in the spiritual realm. The peace they can get is never permanent. Their torment resumes all the more.

Life is fundamentally spiritual; therefore, lasting transformation requires engagement with the spiritual realm through an alliance with Jesus Christ, who holds supreme authority and power over all creation. (Ephesians 1 verse 22).

In every town and village he went to, Jesus taught, delivered, and healed. He never sent a person away with his infirmity or oppression.

Peter will bear witness to Jesus' determination to bring the kingdom of God into the lives of men in Cornelius, the Roman centurion:

Acts 10 verses 37 to 38; KJV

37 That word, I say, ye know, which was published throughout all Judaea, and began from Galilee, after the baptism which John preached; 38 How God anointed Jesus of Nazareth with the Holy Ghost and with power: who went about doing good, and healing all that were oppressed of the devil; for God was with him.

From the perspective of the Holy Spirit, sickness is an oppression of the devil. Unless we see the sick and infirm as prisoners whom Satan tortures, we will not have the right attitude to exercise authority.

Jesus said of the woman who had carried an infirmity for eighteen years and who walked hunched over that it was Satan who had bound her during all these years. Woman, you are free from your infirmity—these were the words he said when he laid his hands on her (Luke 13 verses 10 to 17).

One day, he went to see Simon Peter, whose mother-in-law had a violent fever. Jesus Christ looked at her and threatened the fever that left her (Luke 4 verses 38 to 39). The spirit causing the fever, or that which oppresses the body must yield to the authority of Jesus.

Ignorance is not good for anyone. We are being defeated

because we do not understand what God did on the cross through Jesus Christ.

Jesus Christ is the last Adam. He is the head of a new breed of men who are called to walk in the dimension of God. Everything Jesus spoke and acted upon served as guidance for us. He exemplified the essence of being a child of God, embodying the life to which the Father has called us.

The Holy Spirit comments on the wonder of the crowd, who had just witnessed the healing of a paralytic, saying that the crowd was glorifying God, who had given men such power (Matthew 9:8).

It is not only to Jesus that authority over the devil has been given, but it is indeed to all the sons of God.

That is why, from the beginning, he will call men to have them with him and to send them to preach and heal the sick.

The making and sending of disciples

Matthew 10 verses 1, 7, and 8; KJV

1 And when he had called unto him his twelve disciples, he gave them power against unclean spirits, to cast them out, and to heal all manner of sickness and all

> manner of disease. [...] 7 And as ye go, preach, saying, The kingdom of heaven is at hand. 8 Heal the sick, cleanse the lepers, raise the dead, cast out devils: freely ye have received, freely give.

It is a spiritual law: the presence of God accompanies everyone He sends. This follows from another spiritual law which proclaims that the Spirit of God comes and overshadows whoever God chooses.

Hence, the one who is sent has been chosen. And if he has been chosen, the Holy Spirit will come to equip him. In fact, it was never God's intention for humans to undertake divine work using human strategies and resources.

Just as God was in Jesus to do his work, he comes to us in the person of his Spirit to fulfill the mandate that he entrusts to us. Our part is to submit our whole being to Him.

He was constantly talking to them about the kingdom of God because it is our Father's house. That's where we belong. It is also through the principles of that dimension that we are called to function.

He taught them the importance of self-denial, the value of sacrifice, intimacy with God, the power of prayer, etc. It is necessary to know God's ways to be able to collaborate effectively with His Spirit.

Therefore, when he stands on the Mount of Olives on the day he ascends to heaven, he will command them to make disciples of all nations and ensure they teach the doctrines he has instructed them in.

Matthew 28 verses 19 to 20; KJV

19 Go ye therefore, and teach all nations, baptizing them in the name of the Father, and of the Son, and of the Holy Ghost: 20 Teaching them to observe all things whatsoever I have commanded you: and, lo, I am with you always, even unto the end of the world. Amen.

Nobody will invent another path. Jesus is the model that comes down from heaven. We must put all our efforts into discovering the things he prescribed in order to put them into practice.

Can we really achieve the results he achieved if we neglect his example? Inventing another path, adding or subtracting—are these not ways of despising God? Can man change the Word of God that is established in heaven forever? Shouldn't he just submit like Jesus, who we are following, did?

A disciple is a person who follows a master. If Jesus is Master and Lord, it is up to us to follow him.

Someone will say: But how do I know if I really follow Jesus?

Those who are led by the Holy Spirit are sons of God (Romans 8:14). Those who strive to obey the Word that the Holy Spirit revealed in the Scriptures will walk in the footsteps of Jesus.

Practical life application of spiritual principles yields the most significant transformation, yet the contemporary Church suffers primarily from a lack of authentic spiritual models who demonstrate these principles in action. Paul said: be imitators of me as I am of Christ (1 Corinthians 11 verse 1).

Almost thirty-one years have passed since the time when I solemnly gave my life to Jesus. I did not have many opportunities to work closely with people who taught and carried out the ministry of deliverance and healing.

If it is true that the prophetic word we have in the 66 books surpasses in value all the visions and the closeness of people who do like Jesus, it is also true that sometimes it is easier to grasp a lesson if you see it being shaped before your eyes.

The Holy Spirit lends us support, guiding those who hunger and thirst for righteousness into God's realm. Should we desire our lives to be in harmony with God's word, the Holy Spirit will pave the way for our growth.

To implement these spiritual principles effectively, we must first assess our current spiritual position and then systematically apply the revelations we have received through divine guidance. It is through faith that we expel demons, through faith that we speak in new tongues, and it is by faith that we heal the sick and prophesy.

The introduction of the Holy Spirit

Isaiah 63:10; KJV

But they rebelled, and vexed his holy Spirit: therefore he was turned to be their enemy, and he fought against them.

He was with God from the beginning. Present at creation, we see Him everywhere in the scriptures, acting in the lives of those whom God had chosen to fulfill His purposes. It was He who made the ministry of Jesus glorious and fruitful. He is the supreme head of the Church on earth.

The Spirit of God had accompanied Moses in his mission in Egypt and then from Egypt in the desert to the plains of Moab, where he had laid his hands on Joshua to be his successor. If the Holy Spirit can be sad, that's proof that he has feelings.

Having been dishonored, the Holy Spirit chose to fight them — he closed the gates of the promised land to the rebels. Someone who has feelings and is capable of making decisions is a person.

Speaking of Him, Jesus said that He will lead us into all the truth. He is speaking. He said what he heard. He heralds things to come. He glorifies Jesus. All of these action verbs apply to a person endowed with intelligence, and will.

> **John 16:13-15; KJV**
>
> 13 Howbeit when he, the Spirit of truth, is come, he will guide you into all truth: for he shall not speak of himself; but whatsoever he shall hear, that shall he speak: and he will shew you things to come. 14 He shall glorify me: for he shall receive of mine, and shall shew it unto you. 15 All things that the Father hath are mine: therefore said I, that he shall take of mine, and shall shew it unto you.

How would you feel if the people you live with didn't care about you? What if they did not take into account your values, your dreams, and your expectations? Surely, we would not feel valued and loved. And we may not be able to give our all to these people.

Such is the situation in which anyone who does not recognize the Holy Spirit as a fully-fledged person who wants to be recognized and valued places himself. He wants to be recognized as the Other Comforter. The Holy Spirit must be for Christians what Jesus was for his followers.

We cannot ignore the One whom Jesus introduced as his Successor on earth and in the Church. We cannot invent another path. Let us develop our intimacy with the Holy Spirit.

The coming of the Holy Spirit and His ministry

Baptism in the Holy Spirit

Acts 9 verse 17; KJV

And Ananias went his way, and entered into the house; and putting his hands on him said, Brother Saul, the Lord, even Jesus, that appeared unto thee in the way as thou camest, hath sent me, that thou mightest receive thy sight, and be filled with the Holy Ghost.

Paul was in a time of consecration; it had been three days since he met the Lord Jesus. Ananias comes on behalf of the Lord Jesus to lay his hands on him so that he can regain his sight and be filled with the Holy Spirit.

Whoever is called and sent must be endowed with power from above. This principle is reflected in all scriptures. Those to whom the construction of the Tabernacle had been entrusted had been endowed with the power of the Holy Spirit. Kings, prophets, and priests were anointed for the same reason.

Ten days after leaving the earth, Jesus sent the Holy Spirit over his 120 disciples, gathered in the upper room, where they awaited the promise in prayer (Acts 1 verses 12 to 14). He told them: you will receive power, the Holy Spirit coming upon you, and you will be my witnesses in Jerusalem, in all Judea, in Samaria, and to the ends of the earth (Acts 1 verse 8).

It is God's plan to fill everyone who believes in the gospel of Christ with His Spirit (Acts 2 verses 37-39). This is why Paul is asking the Ephesian disciples, who presumably did not have the mark of those who are anointed. Did you receive the Holy Spirit when you believed? (Acts 19 verse 2)

Paul learned from the Lord Jesus to build the faith of his people on the power of God and not on persuasive discourses of human wisdom. Imitating Jesus, he based his preaching on a demonstration of Spirit and power (1 Corinthians 2 verses 4 to 5).

Just as Paul was chosen by Jesus to serve His purposes and was endowed with power, Jesus desires to empower each one of us similarly. The conquest of territories (Jerusalem, Judea, Samaria, the end of the world) is possible only if one has received power from above.

Let's follow Paul's example, let's dedicate ourselves. Let us cry out to Jesus our desire to access the abundant life of God. The Holy Spirit will be able to give us precise instructions, as he did with Ananias.

Manifestations of the Holy Spirit

1 Corinthians 12:4 to 7 ; KJV

4 Now there are diversities of gifts, but the same Spirit. 5 And there are differences of administrations, but the same Lord. 6 And there are diversities of operations, but it is the same God which worketh all in all. 7 But the manifestation of the Spirit is given to every man to profit withal.

The manifestations of the Holy Spirit are varied. It equips all those to whom Jesus entrusts service. Our Father is the One who works everything in all. Its supreme aim is to put everything under the dominion of Jesus. If we accept the call that he is giving us, we must take up all the weapons that he gives us.

The Holy Spirit and its manifestations are our first asset. He sees what we don't see. He knows what we don't know. And he plans so that we may be victorious in the battles we have to fight to establish the kingdom of God.

The kingdom of God must be established in our lives and in the places where he sends us. We need to start battles on his behalf and win them. Jesus' radius of influence must be constantly growing.

1 Corinthians 12:8 to 11 ; KJV

8 For to one is given by the Spirit the word of wisdom; to another the word of knowledge by the same Spirit; 9 To another faith by the same Spirit; to another the gifts of healing by the same Spirit; 10 To another the working of miracles; to another prophecy; to another discerning of spirits; to another divers kinds of tongues; to another the interpretation of tongues: 11 But all these worketh that one and the selfsame Spirit, dividing to every man severally as he will.

It is according to our calling that the Holy Spirit equips us. Any Christian can potentially dispense with the above manifestations (gifts) listed here. Depending on the circumstances, the Holy Spirit can use us if we are willing. Faith is at the base of each of them. Without firm assurance that the Father will do what he has promised, we will cut off the flow of the Holy Spirit.

In general, the Holy Spirit will cause some manifestations to be more abundant than others because of our specific calling. But remember that any Christian can potentially dispense all of them. Since He lives within us, He can do what He wants at any time, if we have learned to submit our members to Him.

Category of revelatory manifestations - They reveal something:

The Word of Wisdom: a fraction of the profound things of God that he makes known to us to reveal his plans, and what is to happen. It indicates a direction.

The Word of Knowledge: a fraction of God's infinite knowledge. It focuses primarily on present and past facts.

Discernment of spirits: thorough judgment of the nature of the spirits active in a given situation.

Category of expression manifestations - they say something:

The Prophecy : an inspired statement. It does not contain revelations in their specific/simple form. It is given to edify, encourage, and urge.

Divers kinds of tongues: commonly called "Speaking in tongues" is the expression in language of the spirit of God's mysteries. We talk to God primarily. It is given for the edification of Christians. When you bring a message in language to church, interpretation is required.

Interpretation of tongues : The Holy Spirit allows one person to grasp the meaning of the message that another person is bringing in tongues.

Category of manifestations of power - They do something:

The faith of God: contrary to the measure of faith, it does not develop. It is manifested when the Father wants to enable us to receive a miracle.

The operation of miracles: the manifestation of the Holy Spirit by which God produces powerful acts and wonderful works through us. It modifies, suspends, and controls natural laws.

Healing manifestations: these are the manifestations by which God repairs what is not working well in our body.

Using each of these gifts well breaks the power of the devil and frees the lives of those we minister to. We need all of these events.

A well-established church must demonstrate, as a body, all nine gifts. When you reach this level of maturity, you are a formidable army against the kingdom of darkness.

Let us seek the face of our God to be equipped. We cannot engage in battles without the power of the Holy Spirit. Nobody before us did it. The disciples waited to be filled. The new creation is filled with the Holy Spirit.

Whoever says he is full and shows nothing is surely mistaken. Jesus said : But ye shall receive power, after that the Holy Ghost is come upon you; and ye shall be witnesses unto me both in Jerusalem, and in all Judaea, and in Samaria, and unto the uttermost part of the earth (Acts 1 verse 8; KJV).

If something troubles us, let us go to our God to ask for understanding and to be fulfilled. He wants us to be in the image of Jesus; filled with the Holy Spirit and with strength. These are the sons of God that Creation is waiting to see. Glory be to God, we belong to the generation where God will fulfill this great promise.

As his eyes scour the earth in search of men in whom he will show strength, if you sincerely desire to raise Jesus and walk as he walked, he will find you. Let us be among those whom the Lord finds.

Baptism in the Holy Spirit: Is it necessary to speak in tongues?

There is an observation that is obvious to us when we read the Book of Acts, which talks about the birth of the Church and its growth.

All the stories of immersion in the Holy Spirit reveal that the people who received this grace also spoke in other tongues.

On the day He left the earth, He assured them that those who believed would witness miracles :

> **Acts 16:17 to 18; KJV**
>
> 17 These are the miracles that will accompany those who believe: in my name, they will drive out demons; they will speak in new languages; 18 they will catch snakes; if they drink any lethal drink, it will not harm them; they will lay their hands on the sick, and the sick will be healed.

Thus, "speaking in tongues" is one of the signs that confirms that one has received the doctrine of Christ.

Lack of knowledge is not good for anyone. If we are limited, it is due to ignorance of God's ways. If Jesus' teaching on the Holy Spirit and its manifestations is not properly delivered, Christians will not be able to enter this dimension of their inheritance.

Let us return to the simplicity of the Gospel, and let us not get locked into the confines of the traditions of the institutional or local churches in which we grew up.

Jesus Christ is the same yesterday, today, and forever. He said that rivers of living water will flow from the belly of anyone who believes in Him. He was talking about the Holy Spirit that was poured out on the disciples on the day of Pentecost.

John 7:37 to 39; KJV

the last day, that great day of the feast, Jesus stood and cried, saying, If any man thirst, let him come unto me, and drink. that believeth on me, as the scripture hath said, out of his belly shall flow rivers of living water. 39 (But this spake he of the Spirit, which they that believe on him should receive: for the Holy Ghost was not yet given; because that Jesus was not yet glorified.)

Tongues are primarily given for the benefit of the believer. It is a kind of coded line of communication that allows him to speak to God in a miraculous language that the Holy Spirit created specifically for him.

The miracle is this: although I may not necessarily understand what I am saying, the Holy Spirit who helps us pray makes sure that the words that rise from my heart to come out of my mouth make sense for God.

1 Corinthians 14 verse 2; KJV

or he that speaketh in an unknown tongue speaketh not unto men, but unto God: for no man under-standeth him; howbeit in the spirit he speaketh mysteries

Every time the Father wants to achieve something on Earth, he will make an alliance with a man so that he can proclaim it on Earth. The coming of Jesus, for example, was foretold by several prophets over the course of many years.

The spiritual world works by declaration. We open doors with words that come out of our mouths. We sow, we water, we establish, and we demolish with the Word.

So whoever tells mysteries prophesies things about what God wants to do. He worships God, sometimes he praises him; sometimes he intercedes for others, sometimes he does spiritual warfare, etc.

I thank my God, I speak with tongues more than ye all (1 Corinthians 14 verse 18; KJV).

Prayer life is limited if it does not include the dimension "Prayer in Tongue." If we long to receive, the One who immerses in the Holy Spirit will fill us. Our limitations are often a reflection of our beliefs.

Acts 10 verses 45 to 48; KJV

45 And they of the circumcision which believed were astonished, as many as came with Peter, because that

on the Gentiles also was poured out the gift of the Holy Ghost. 46 For they heard them speak with tongues, and magnify God. Then answered Peter, 47 Can any man forbid water, that these should not be baptized, which have received the Holy Ghost as well as we? 48 And he commanded them to be baptized in the name of the Lord. Then prayed they him to tarry certain days.

Peter and the circumcised faithful (Jews) who accompany him are surprised. This reaction perhaps reflected their deeply ingrained theological presumption of Israel's spiritual preeminence among nations.

Perhaps they had thought that the Father would treat Christians of pagan origin less favorably than Christians of Jewish origin.

Perhaps they thought that heathen people should be subject to some ordinances of the Law of Moses to be entitled to the gift of the Holy Spirit. They are surprised because the Father does not take into account the other factors.

The Word of the Cross holds paramount importance, as does the faith demonstrated in reaction to its proclamation. The 120 followers of Jesus had waited 10 days, in the upper room, to see the Holy Spirit come down. The 3000 converts on the day of Pentecost had been immersed in water, and hands had been laid upon them to receive the Holy Spirit.

In Samaria, after the evangelist Philip made a lot of converts, Peter and John descended from Jerusalem to lay their hands on the new converts. In Cornelius, the Father seems to act differently; immersion in the Holy Spirit is given before immersion in water. This shows us that once a person is born again, they are ready to be filled with the Holy Spirit. Whoever meets the conditions can have both experiences practically at the same time.

Peter and the Jewish Christians who accompany him conclude that Cornelius and his guests were immersed in the Holy Spirit because they heard them speak in other languages. Whoever has been immersed in the Holy Spirit speaks in other tongues.

The growth process

2 Corinthians 3 verses 17 to 18; KJV

17 Now the Lord is that Spirit: and where the Spirit of the Lord is, there is liberty. 18 But we all, with open face beholding as in a glass the glory of the Lord, are changed into the same image from glory to glory, even as by the Spirit of the Lord.

Those who are born of God come into His presence. They went from the Kingdom of Darkness to the Kingdom of Enlightenment. The Spirit of God is given to them as a deposit for their glorious inheritance, which is in heaven.

What is the mission of the Holy Spirit given to the child of God?

- Leading the child of God into all the truth
- Repeat to the child of God the things he has heard from the Father
- Tell him about things to come
- Glorifying Jesus
- Take what is Jesus' and give it to God's child

John 16:13 to 15; KJV

13 Howbeit when he, the Spirit of truth, is come, he will guide you into all truth: for he shall not speak of himself; but whatsoever he shall hear, that shall he speak: and he will shew you things to come. 14 He shall glorify me: for he shall receive of mine, and shall shew it unto you. 15 All things that the Father hath are mine: therefore said I, that he shall take of mine, and shall shew it unto you.

The Holy Spirit is given to bring us from childhood to maturity in Jesus. It starts with intimacy with God. This is the meaning of the expression "to contemplate the face of the Lord" that we find in 2 Corinthians 3:18.

Intimacy

In the past, access to God was reserved only for priests who had been separated from the people. They could only enter the Holy Place. Only the High Priest could go to the Most Holy Place once a year.

Moses, on the other hand, had unlimited access to the presence of God. He had been honored to learn more and more about God's ways. As a result, he was continuously transformed to serve his God more effectively.

The encounter with the burning bush had changed her life. No one can see the face of God and remain the same. It is in its light that we see the light. He is the God who reveals to man why he was created.

Moses was chosen to be the apostle of the Old Covenant. His encounter with God in the desert marked the beginning of his introduction to his calling. Through subsequent meetings with the Father, he was firmly established in his role.

Similarly, Abram was created to be Abraham — the Father of many. The model of justice that is obtained through faith. The one through whom the Seed of the woman will come. The one through whom all the nations of the earth are blessed.

Abram's growing closeness to God changed his life. He experienced the glory of God because he allowed himself to be transformed.

When Jesus died on the cross, the veil in the temple that divided the Holy of Holies from the Holy Place was torn in two by the angels of God. With the price of sin paid, access to God's presence is now limitless for anyone who comes through. the Cross.

Hebrews 10 verses 19 to 23; KJV

19 Having therefore, brethren, boldness to enter into the holiest by the blood of Jesus, 20 By a new and living way, which he hath consecrated for us, through the veil, that is to say, his flesh; 21 And having an high priest over the house of God; 22 Let us draw near with a true heart in full assurance of faith, having our hearts sprinkled from an evil conscience, and our bodies washed with pure water. 23 Let us hold fast the profession of our faith without wavering; (for he is faithful that promised;)

We are the assistants of Jesus, who is now serving as high priest in the temple that is in heaven. We approach through prayer and meditation on the Word. They work powerfully in us in collaboration with fellowship and service to make us mature in Christ.

Intimate proximity to God enables clear spiritual vision; through dwelling in His presence, we gain comprehensive understanding of His nature and character. From God's revelation comes knowledge of our identity and our calling.

As theologian John Owen argues in his seminal work on pneumatology, the Holy Spirit's operative power extends throughout the entirety of the believer's spiritual journey (Owen, "Pneumatologia" 234). He brings us into the presence of God, where we can contemplate His majesty, His magnificence, and His glory.

The revelation of His love impels us to reject everything that does not come from Him. In place of what is taken away, we receive the treasures of heaven. We are transformed into his image to experience even greater and more valuable things.

Metanoïa

Luke 3 verses 4 to 6; KJV

4 As it is written in the book of the words of Esaias the prophet, saying, The voice of one crying in the wilderness, Prepare ye the way of the Lord, make his paths straight.5 Every valley shall be filled, and every mountain and hill shall be brought low; and the crooked shall be made straight, and the rough ways shall be made smooth; 6 And all flesh shall see the salvation of God.

Μετάνοια (metanoia), the Greek term traditionally translated as "repentance," carries deeper connotations of transformative thinking. John the Baptist is the one who speaks in the preceding verses.

He preached repentance. It is a non-negotiable prerequisite for the manifestation of God's glory.

Many people refuse to understand that life is spiritual. It is governed by spiritual laws that flow from the Word of God, which is established forever in heaven. God, who has achieved everything through Jesus, has entered into his rest. The victory of the Cross will be manifested in the life of every man who fulfills the conditions of the promise that he has appropriated.

But we must become the promise within us in order for it to be manifested outside. The thing will not come as we have often thought to us. It will come through us. We are changed to be the conduit through which what we want comes.

Are we starting to see the importance of "Metanoïa"? Whoever really wants to see the glory of God will cry out day and night: Father, show me the paths to be smoothed out in my life. Valleys to fill, mountains and hills to lower, tortuous things to straighten, rough roads to smooth out.

You have to renounce yourself to become a disciple. You must continue to die to yourself and to the things of the world to become a consummate follower.

The Word of God is the rule. Anything that does not conform to the line the Word of God draws is inequity. Justice is the state of what follows the line perfectly. The Holy Spirit will put his finger on the things that need to be removed.

Those who were born of God died to the world. They are not of the world. They don't like the world or the things that are in it. They are more and more in the image of their Father who is Holy.

How will they be formidable gates to heaven if they continue to think and act like the people of this world ?

In the same way that the one who stops progressing has begun to regress, it is by being transformed by the renewal of our intelligence that we move ever higher on the spiritual growth ladder.

In my own life and in the lives of many people I have met, I have seen the power of repentance. The sooner the Lord changes our way of thinking, the more quickly we will grow in the things of God.

Whoever loves his life as it is will remain outside of God's greatest and most precious promises. The call to walk in the dimension of God is for everyone.

Glory

Psalm 145 verses 11 to 12; KJV

11 They shall speak of the glory of thy kingdom, and talk of thy power; 12 To make known to the sons of men his mighty acts, and the glorious majesty of his kingdom.

Glory: From the Hebrew word "kabowd" - abundance, honor, splendor, reputation, dignity of the position; relating to external conditions and circumstances. In the New Testament, it is translated from the Greek word "dóksa"—honor, fame, tacit manifestation of God, splendor.

The glory of God is his reputation, his dignity, and his splendor. It is the manifestation of his greatness and power, of the weight of his presence in any place. Whether he is in his temple or coming down to visit men on earth, our God, who is also the greatest of all kings, moves with an impressive procession of angels.

After three days of preparation, the people who had just come out of Egypt witnessed the coming of Yahweh on Mount Sinai. On the third day in the morning, there was thunder, lightning, and a thick cloud on the mountain; the sound of the trumpet was heard loudly; and all the people who were in the camp were seized of terror (Exodus 19 verse 16). There was an all-consuming fire at the top of the mountain that was shaking violently (Exodus 19 Verse 18).

A few days later, Yahweh brought up to Him not only Moses, Aaron, Nadab, and Abihu, his sons, but also the seventy elders of Israel (Exodus 24 verse 1). They went up to Him after an altar had been built and the covenant between Jehovah and His people had been sealed. They saw the God of Israel; under his feet, it was like a transparent work of sapphire, like heaven itself in its purity (Exodus 24 verse 10).

Yahweh wants to be known by men, especially by his people.

In Egypt, he made his glory shine by performing wonders. Pharaoh's magicians, who had mimicked the miracles performed by Moses, were forced to recognize the supremacy of Yahweh (Exodus 8 verses 16-19). Pharaoh did the same when Egypt's first-born children were killed and his entire army was destroyed.

All proclaim his greatness and power when he shines forth his glory by performing wonders on earth. The Lord wants to be recognized as God by those he created for his glory. This is why, in Jesus' teaching on prayer, the name, the kingdom and the glory of God are the first elements mentioned: Our Father which art in heaven, Hallowed be thy name. Thy kingdom come. Thy will be done in earth, as it is in heaven. (Matthew 6:9-10).

He shows his glory by doing wonders in our lives. He also shows it by introducing us into his presence. Whoever has seen the glory of God asks for more. Moses said: Show me your glory (Exodus 33 verse 18). Our body should be protected from the weight of God's glory when he shows it. Yahweh put Moses in a rock as he passed by to show him the glory of God. He covered it with his hand to protect him (Exodus 33:22).

The Holy Spirit came to bring us into the glory of God. As the son of God, his glory is where we live. The more we are aware of it, the more successful our walk is. For he has called us to his kingdom and glory (1 Thessalonians 2 verse 12).

4

Testimonies of healings and deliverances

Mark 16 verses 15 to 20; KJV

15 And he said unto them, Go ye into all the world, and preach the gospel to every creature. 16 He that believeth and is baptized shall be saved; but he that believeth not shall be damned. 17 And these signs shall follow them that believe; In my name shall they cast out devils; they shall speak with new tongues; 18 They shall take up serpents; and if they drink any deadly thing, it shall not hurt them; they shall lay hands on the sick, and they shall recover. 19 So then after the Lord had spoken unto them, he was received up into heaven, and sat on the right hand of God. 20 And they went forth, and preached every where, the Lord working with them, and confirming the word with signs following. Amen.

The normal Christian life is supernatural. He recreated us in Jesus so that we could be partakers of his glory. The Lord is in the midst of his people, and he takes pleasure in confirming the Word that we proclaim.

When it comes to miracles and wonders, Satan is capable of doing them. Hinduists, Buddhists, Muslims, followers of Jewish mysticism, the Kabbalah, followers of various mystical orders, Satanists, and sorcerers are all capable of working miracles. Man can become the channel of forces that are not of the physical dimension of which we are most aware.

If the Spirit of God is called the Holy Spirit, it is also because everything that is outside of Him is not holy. What is the point we want to make? Miracles and wonders are not enough to prove that we are in the presence of a manifestation that comes from the living God who manifested Himself to men in the person of Jesus Christ.

The dreams, visions, prophecies, sermons, and all the declarations that men make in the name of God cannot be received if they deviate even a little from the Scriptures. Paul testified of the things he saw and heard (visions) without departing from Moses and the prophets (designation of the scriptures) — Acts 26 verse 22.

Paul said to the Galatians: But though we, or an angel from heaven, preach any other gospel unto you than that which we have preached unto you, let him be accursed (Galatians 1 verse 8). Peter, who saw the glory of the transfigured Jesus in the company of Moses and Elijah, placed the prophetic word (The

Scriptures) above this vision — which is the solid foundation on which God builds our lives and His Church (2 Peter 1 verse 18 to 19).

Madame Elisabeth, recovering from a sore knee

We were attending a divine healing conference in Toronto. At the time of the prayer for the sick, the speaking couple asked those who had any need to raise their hands; and those who had the Holy Spirit to pray for them. I spoke to Madame Elizabeth, who was sitting behind us, because she had raised her hand. She told me that she had knee pain that restricted her movements. I put my hand on his knee to pray: cursing the root and source of the infirmity; cursing the pain; taking authority over the tendons, muscles, cartilage, etc., and asking the Lord to put back anything that was missing in its place. The joy on Madame Elizabeth's face confirmed what she had told me: I no longer feel pain; everything is fine.

Madame Berthe freed from a language difficulty

Hugo is a faithful servant of the Lord Jesus who practices healing and deliverance. Entering the office of one of his managers this morning, he noticed a woman who had great difficulty expressing herself. Guided by the Holy Spirit, he approached Madame Berthe, placed his hand on her head, and called upon God's grace.

When the lady found him outside the office on her way home, she thanked him for the healing she had received.

He said: they will lay their hands on the sick and the sick will be healed.His motivation stemmed from the desire to free that oppressed woman from her shackles.

Let us develop the habit of laying hands on the sick in the name of Jesus. He wants to touch them.

Madame Tana recovered from an appalling chest pain

I was sitting at my desk a few weeks ago when the Holy Spirit wanted me to contact Mrs. Tana to get the latest news. I chose an asynchronous communication mode. To my surprise, she returned my text message. She was not supposed to be up at this time due to the time difference. I learned that she was going through some pretty difficult times at the family level.

After calling her to find out more, she told me that she had had chest pain since morning.

The context of the latest family events made her fear a mystical attack. She had no desire to fall asleep. I understood why the Holy Spirit had led me to call her. After about ten minutes of intense prayer, the pain was gone. Jesus Christ had completely freed her.

Mrs. B., recovered from a throbbing back pain

We had just finished a meeting and I was walking in the middle of the crowd to recognize, greet, and encourage this or that one. While talking to Mrs. B., she told me about the presence of an appalling pain in her back — the kind of pain that people try to ignore in order to live normally.

Having called on another person who was nearby, we prayed in the name of Jesus by laying our hands on the lady. Jesus gave peace to Mrs. B. — The pain was gone.

The Lord is merciful and compassionate. He is looking for ways and means to deliver those who are oppressed in various ways by the devil.

Mr. Siba, freed from the spirits that oppressed him

It was a Saturday afternoon and I was in my office when I was interrupted by a call from a number I did not recognize. At the end of the phone, a young man identified himself and asked me if we were practicing deliverance. I answered him in the affirmative. He told me that he urgently needed help. I suggested that he meet me at the church at 5 pm.

When he finished telling me a short version of his story, I understood that he had been off work for several months, that he was constantly oppressed by impure spirits who wanted to drive him to commit suicide.

After about forty minutes of prayer for deliverance, Mr. Siba looked better. It felt light. Full of joy, he spoke of getting his life back on track. Jesus had expelled the impure spirits that troubled him.

A few days later, he had found a job and the joy of being able to take care of himself. The projects that he had stopped all seemed possible to him again.

Madame S., recovered from the absence of sensation in her right thigh

With each manifestation, the Father has let us know a particular aspect of his power. We continue to learn about deliverance and healing. Here, it was a question of understanding that we do not need to physically lay hands on a person for Jesus to operate.

It was a Wednesday, we were praising the Lord before the Bible study phase in the church we attended for seven years before starting our ministry.

At the end of the worship, Mrs. S. testified that she felt movements in her right leg during the worship time and that she had regained sensitivity. None of us laid our hands on her, except the angels of our Lord.

Praise brings about the active presence of God. Healing and deliverance occur in the lives of those who are prepared in their hearts.

Many have not yet understood the importance of praise and worship. Sometimes they will come to the service just in time to listen to the message, not understanding that they are missing the most important moment: the moment when we come up to His presence to tell Him our passion. Important transactions take place during these blessed times.

The Holy Spirit taught us to take the moment of worship very seriously. We take all the time we need to go up, to build a throne for Him, to hear His decrees and to proclaim them here.

Mr. G., recovered from a heart valve problem

It was a Saturday that I went to the hospital to visit Mr. G. who had just had heart surgery, which had not solved the problem. There was no question of making another attempt to fix the problem of a leaking valve. The success rate of such a procedure was approximately 15%, given the situation and his age.

It was therefore decided that once his condition had stabilized, he would go to a nursing home for seniors. After an exchange of about thirty minutes, I asked him to pray for his heart and for her legs that had weakened. Then, I suggested that he get out of bed and take a short walk of about thirty steps affirming the reign of Jesus in his body. Having brought him back to bed, I left.

A woman who was in the same room and who was suffering

from cancer objected to my praying for her by saying: Do you really think I'm going to get better? - I answered with a smile: Jesus can heal you.

At the beginning of the week, I received the news that Mr. G. was going to be released by his doctors who did not understand what had happened. Jesus had given him the heart of a nineteen-year-old young man, according to doctors' comments. The man whose life was going downhill had regained his means and autonomy. Jesus is faithful.

Mrs. Petrosi, recovered from a leg problem and weight loss

The story takes place in the season when the Holy Spirit was teaching me about healing. As I watched videos of past evangelists on the Internet, the desire to get into these things grew. Lord, are these things for everyone? — A.A. Allen said in one of these videos: miracles will accompany those who believe.

On the way to go to Mrs. Petrosi, who had told me about her multiple ailments, I prayed in tongue all the way.

The trip takes about an hour. She suffered from leg pain and could not see the specialists for at least four months. The Holy Spirit convinced me that this was my opportunity to practice what I had seen on video (A.A. Allen, Kathryn Kulman, Jack Coe, A.W. Schamback, Benny Hinn, etc.).

That day, I asked Mrs. Petrosi to pray for her leg. Having put my hand down, I had not prayed for fifteen seconds for my hand to heat up, and I saw her in tears because the pain was gone. She said that everything was fine.

Mrs. Petrosi stopped using the electric chair, which made it easier for her to move around. And over the next few weeks, she lost about 20 pounds. Jesus saved his life from the oppression of the Devil. For the first time, I saw Jesus do it right in front of my eyes — it was no longer through videos.

Let us dare to offer our members to Jesus (Romans 12 verse 1). If we learn to not be self-aware, He will be able to do great things throughout our lives.

Dave, Word of Knowledge (Healing) and Night Visions

God is no respecter of persons. Wherever there are people who want to see his glory, he shows up with power.

In the three testimonies that follow, Dave encourages us to expect Jesus to respond to our desire to experience spiritual things.

<u>Word of knowledge and headache healing</u>

We had just had a seminar on prophetic ministry and the

gifts of prophecy. This teaching has truly revolutionized my understanding of these various topics and has inspired in me a thirst to see the Lord use me in His work. A few days into the course, as I was working, I was suddenly struck by a severe headache.

Wanting to exercise the authority that the Lord gave me, I began to put my hand on my head to quell this pain. As I was doing it, I heard the Holy Spirit tell me that it was not about me, it was about someone else.

I then looked around and looked for someone who had a headache. Nobody in my physical environment seemed to be affected. I then contacted everyone with whom I had an exchange by phone, but so far, nothing.

So I made the decision to pray, even though I don't know who it is, in the belief that the Lord would touch the person wherever they were. After a few minutes, I saw the picture of a person with whom I had spoken that day, but I had not thought of her when I contacted those with whom I had spoken by phone.

So I asked her if she had a headache during the day, the answer was yes, and I asked if the pain was still present, she said no, and I asked when the pain went away, and that was when I prayed, not knowing who I was praying for.

<u>God speaks through dreams</u>

I dreamed that I was with a young friend from the church in

New Bell, she was asking me questions about faith. She was surprised at how well I knew God's word and told me about her desire to know more about the Lord.

In the morning, I called this friend to explain my dream to her, and she let me know that it was exactly her prayer to know the Lord better and to devote herself to him. I guided her to the various things that helped me grow in the things of the Lord.

God reveals the status of a file submitted to an administration.

I was in the process of applying for residence for Canada. We were on our 21-day program of fasts and prayers. Before going to bed, I asked the Lord for showing me the things I need to know. At night, I saw that there was a "rejection" mention on my immigration file, even though it was in compliance.

I got up in the morning to pray against it and during the day, I called immigration to follow up on my file, and they let me know that the system did indeed put a rejection on my file, but it was a mistake and they were going to correct it, which was done.

Lionel freed from an appalling headache

One evening, when I came home from work, exhausted after a long day, a painful ache came over me. Driving on a dark road, I felt my vision blurring, as if wrapped in a veil of pain. These migraines, which were slight at first, quickly turned into an oppressive torment, making every second behind the wheel an ordeal.

Fatigue and pain mixed, making every thought confusing. However, in the midst of this chaos, an idea came to me: to pray. But to my surprise, the more I prayed, the more the pain seemed to intensify, as a challenge to my faith. It was as if these migraines wanted me to bend under their weight.

Struggling with the pain, I closed my eyes for a moment and suddenly heard a soft but powerful voice of the Holy Spirit. She asked me to take authority and curse these migraines.

Suddenly, incredible courage and strength came over me. It was as if a divine light had lit up inside me, dispelling the darkness and the pain. With a conviction that I had never felt before, I started threatening these migraines, ordering them to leave me in the powerful name of Jesus.

And then, like a miracle, the pain disappeared. Instantly. A freshness came over me, a feeling of lightness made me float in my car. I was free, not only from physical pain, but also from a spiritual burden. My lips then opened to praise the Lord with all my heart, singing his praises for his incomparable benefits.

That evening, I experienced the power of Jesus Christ in a tangible and profound way. He reminded me that in every trial, no matter how great, His name is a fortress, a refuge, and an inexhaustible source of healing and peace. May all the glory go to Him, our Savior and Eternal King.

Olivier and Liliane, the power of God in marriage

My name is Liliane and I have been married to Olivier since 2015.

We got married and thought we knew God, but we lived very far away from him.

In practice, I read the Bible from time to time and went to church every Sunday without exception, but on the other side, I always went to nightclubs and watched all kinds of movies without exception.

When we had our second daughter, it was a shock for me, as she was born very premature (29 weeks) and very ill. Her chances of survival were slim. I cried to God pleading with him to save her. I promised Him that I would seek Him with all my heart.

God in His love, saved our daughter, and we called her Mboutni, which means Blessing, because that's what she was, a blessing. In fact, by saving her, God also brought my heart back to Him.

In 2017, I experienced a rebirth, taught myself to read the Bible, and opened my heart to the teachings of the Holy Spirit, gaining a true understanding of what it means to be a child of God.

My prayer was therefore directed at my husband, Olivier, because I wanted him to meet Jesus too.

It took many years of strife between us, but God, in His love, taught me to be submissive and to build my home on Jesus alone.

I made choices that went against what my husband wanted, but it was because I obeyed my Dad, who is in heaven, and for that, he rewarded me in the most beautiful way.

In 2019, we had our first boy (and third child), and God visited me in a dream to reveal that he would give me another son and that his name would be Noah the year after.

I told my husband and sister about my dream, and they said they didn't believe it. It was probably because I had just given birth.

The next year, when we celebrated 1 year of Nkoni, the first boy, and when we were not expecting it at all, I conceived our second boy right away – The Lord was unbeknownst to us what I had seen in my dream.

Olivier had a truly incredible 2020. There was the COVID pandemic and the lockdown. For many couples, it was hard, but for us, it was a blessing.

My husband and I had never spent more than three months in the same house (he was called upon to commute a lot at work), so some people around me asked me how this was going and would happen.

This was going quite well, and as a bonus, in prayer, submission, and confession, the Spirit of the Lord touched my husband once again, and since this year we have a new family, a new couple, and a new home. We are united before God spiritually.

Noah was conceived and born in 2020, as the Lord had me announce, and it marked the time my husband met Jesus. The name Noah makes perfect sense, because the Lord made a new covenant with us; it was a new beginning.

We bless the Lord for saving us and we are convinced that through us, he will touch many people as well.

Through this testimony, we want to urge couples not to become discouraged when we wait for a response from God, but to persevere in prayer, because God loves us and wants to see us live a life of fullness.

Nathalie, recovered from hypothyroidism

Beloved in the Lord Good morning. I am Nathalie, the mother of several children. I have come to give my testimony to glorify the name of Jesus. I have been a child of God for several years now. I confessed and accepted Jesus as my Savior and Lord. And I went through baptism by immersion.

It's been roughly a year since I recovered from an illness that had been afflicting me for several years.

I am the mother of several children. Some time after the birth of my first son, I began to gain weight considerably. Since he was my first son, I attributed it to motherhood. Following consultations with the doctor and numerous examinations, it was concluded that this was not normal.

In 2011, I was diagnosed with a problem with my thyroid gland. It was faulty. I had hypothyroidism. I was gaining weight. I had a problem with hormones. It was madness in my body. Nothing was holding up.

Following this diagnosis, my family doctor prescribed Synthroid - the medication I needed to take to correct the problem with my thyroid gland. So I took this medication for several years. I kept praying about it. And every time we prayed for the sick, I cried out to God: Deliver me. I was a very thin person. I had almost never had a weight problem ; I had hardly ever had a weight or hormone problem. Then, my first son, everything turned upside down. It was really crazy in my body: the hormones, the weight, the thyroid—it was really complicated.

I cried out to God because I no longer recognized myself. I didn't recognize my body anymore. I did not understand what was happening to me.

I said to myself: Oh God, if that's it to have children... if having children is to get high like that, it's because... I was discouraged.

And things were getting complicated. The more time passed, the more complicated things got. But I was still taking Synthroid. The doctor kept increasing the doses that I took as the years went by. They increased the strength of the drug: 50 mcg, 75 mcg, etc.

And then I became pregnant with my second child — it must be said that it was very difficult for me to have it, given the hormonal instability in which my body found itself. It is a miracle baby whose conception will be the subject of another testimony to the glory of Jesus.

I was still carrying around this hypothyroidism disease. I was already almost in year 6 of the disease. And I've always taken Synthroid. During pregnancy, the doses had to be increased due to the child growing inside me and my body's inability to provide all the hormones needed.

I kept praying, praying, praying. At one point, I was desperate because the doctor told me that taking Synthroid was for life.

I had had this disease for six years. After the birth of the second child, things were not getting better. On the contrary, they have worsened. I was swelling; I was gaining weight; I was struggling to lose weight; I was doing physical exercises ; I was on diets. I did all sorts of business. One shot, and I'm losing the weight; all of a sudden, I'm regaining the weight; it was madness in my body. Nothing was working. And the moods... the hormones... everything... it didn't work.

Even the doctor saw my determination to lose weight. I really wanted to lose weight. I didn't want this body anymore.

I don't want to say that I hated my body, but I didn't like what I saw in the mirror. I tried not to dwell on my image.

And I kept crying out to God: Lord, no, that's not me. I don't recognize this body that I am in. What is wrong, Lord? — Deliver me, deliver me.

As I cried out to God, the Lord revealed to me more about His faithfulness and what He is able to do for me.

It is important to note that before my first son came in 2011, I did not know the Lord. I was a simple, good girl who loved doing her own thing. I knew that God was there, that he cared for us, and that he existed; but I had no relationship with that God.

So, as I said above, I am giving birth to my son and my health is starting to play tricks on me. In the meantime, I am really meeting this great God. I am developing this relationship with Him. I am walking with Him. I am growing up with Him.

And as time goes by, I understand that this God really wants to heal me; I understand that he is able to heal me. So I really trusted in God.

One of the first things I asked God to do was get rid of hypothyroidism. It must be said that it was not the only thing that tired me. I will talk about the other deliverance in future testimonies. I am really someone to whom I have done a lot of good. It healed me of all sorts of ailments.

I was afflicted with illness, and the Lord Jesus quietly liberated me from all these conditions, including hypothyroidism, which I am now testifying about.

So, I am evolving with the Lord. I am holding his hand and he is holding my hand. I am walking with Him. He reveals to me in his Word that he is the God who heals. He reveals to me that by his bruises, I was healed. He reveals to me through the Holy Spirit, who walked with me and is now with me, that he is the God who delivers me. I believe in that and then I keep praying, but I don't see the result.

Time goes by, and I give birth to my third child. And I am still trapped in this disease. I keep crying out to God: Lord, when will my miracle come out. I am tired.

My family doctor tells me: let go because you are going to take Synthroid for the rest of your life. So Synthroid was my friend. I didn't go anywhere without Synthroid. I had to take one tablet in the morning.

From 2011, the year I had my first child, to 2020, the year I had my third baby, I had to take Synthroid every morning. And the doses kept increasing. I was tired Sometimes I would stop taking it out of anger. As soon as things got worse—I swelled; the hormones— it was really a disaster. So I always ran back to pick it up again because I understood that I couldn't do anything without Synthroid.

And then the Lord intervened last year (in 2023). Indeed, it has been almost a year since the Lord Jesus cured me of hypothyroidism at one of our church prayer evenings.

I felt something in my body as if stuff were being displaced or put back. It felt like someone was operating on my throat. It started from my throat and went down into my body. I felt that things were being fixed. It's as if there were things that were moved inside me and that they were put back in their place.

And then I felt in my mind that the Lord had healed me. It was clear to me that the Lord was healing me because, before that, I had had dreams where I was throwing away medication. But I did not understand.

It must be said that in our church, the last week of each month is dedicated to fasting and prayer. That week, when I was healed, I said this prayer:

Lord, you are faithful. I know that you are the great God who healed me. So again this week, I am coming back with hypothyroidism. That's not mine; I want you to get rid of it. You can get rid of this for me. I have had this disease for more than ten years—more than ten years that I have been forced to take pills every day of my life. I want you to release me.

I am tired. And the word that says: come to me, you, who are tired and burdened, came into my mind. I got that word.

And I said, God, I am tired of hypothyroidism. I am tired of taking the pills. When I forget to take the pills, it's a problem. I am tired of being condemned to live like this. I want my deliverance. Do me good, Lord; You are capable.

That week, I prayed like that. And the Lord showed me several times in dreams how I was throwing away Synthroid. On the last Friday of that month, we prayed, and I received my healing.

I knew things had happened. I was also a bit doubtful. But I didn't allow my thoughts to be based on negative ideas: I stopped thinking. And I said to myself that I was healed. The enemy wanted me to believe the opposite.

The next day, the Saturday that followed, that prayer evening, I really took a step in faith. Something I had not done in the past. I went to get my Synthroid —I always ordered them for three months. So I always had a big three-month box of Synthroid at my bedside.

I took a step of faith. I went to take the Synthroid exactly as I saw them in my visions, and I went to throw them away. And when I threw it away, I said: Lord, you showed me that I was throwing away these medications because they no longer belong to me; because You cured me of hypothyroidism; because I was in prison for more than ten years of my life and you freed me. I seal my healing in the blood of Jesus.

While throwing, I spoke to the Synthroid, saying: Synthroid, I am done with you. I'll never take it again. You don't have to be in my body anymore. I don't need you. I am healed. It's the end with you today. You have accompanied me for more than ten years of my life; enough is enough. The Lord delivers me from you today. I took the Synthroid and threw it in the trash.

And when I threw it away, I really felt in my spirit that it was over. I didn't throw it away like the other times I refused to take it, and then I ran back to take it because things were getting worse in my body.

The day after prayer Friday, when I woke up, instead of taking the Synthroid — it was the first thing I usually did when I woke up, I took it that time and threw it in the trash.

In the days that followed, I was thankful to the Lord for my healing. The days passed, and I was no longer taking Synthroid. And I did not go for tests. Generally, I liked to validate the things that the Lord was doing in my life. At that time, it was clear in my head that I was not going to validate anything. For me, it was not a question of doing a test to confirm what the Lord had done.

The days have passed; the weeks have passed; the months have passed and I have not taken Synthroid again. I did not see a doctor.

I realized that not only did my thyroid become normal, but I started to lose weight. I could see in my clothes that I was losing weight. My surroundings asked me about what I was doing to get such results. Before, I did sports; I dieted; I put money into all sorts of things to lose weight but to no avail. But now, I no longer have time to practice sports. I didn't have time to invest in the things I used to do to lose weight and it didn't work. And I was still losing weight.

I was someone who was tired all the time, and then I really felt the strength coming back. I felt really good about my body.

The next time I went to the family doctor for my eyes, he was surprised that I had not renewed my prescription for hypothyroidism in a long time. I informed him that I no longer needed it because the Lord Jesus Christ had healed me.

When the doctor heard that I had not taken Synthroid for a year, she said: No, you did not do that... Yes, I did—I retorted. So she began to examine me. I got on the scale for weight gain. And she did a series of checks. Then she sat in her chair, looked at me, and didn't know what to say. Because everything showed that I was fine. There was no longer any sign of hypothyroidism. She was forced to realize that the person she had been following since 2012 was no longer the person who was standing in front of her in 2024. So she said, Wow, the older you get, the better off you are.

As for me, I understood in my spirit: the more I walk with God, the more I know this God, the more I have the revelation that I walk with someone who is all-powerful, and the more I see the hand of God in my life. She agreed with me that I no longer needed Synthroid.

Today, I no longer practice sports to fight something. I do sports for my well-being. I am not trying to escape a disease that has kept me captive for more than 10 years.

I thank the Lord Jesus, who delivered me from hypothyroidism after more than ten years of suffering. Jesus took the Synthroid boxes from my hands and put them in the trash. As a result of this healing, many other healings have taken place in my body.

I am giving this testimony for the glory of My God. May his name be blessed. Amen.

Isaiah Nathan, night vision and the power of the name of Jesus

Well, actually, my dream happened 2 or 3 years ago. I was about 13 or 12 years old. It was during a night like any other. I was in a dimension or a room — a place where there were types of blocks and it was a journey.

In the beginning, I did the game track normally: I climbed, I went down, and I ran. At some point, people showed up and they were chasing me. I understood that it was the devil with his army because I could not see their faces, but I saw that black things were following me from afar. They had horses. I kept running and at one point I tripped. And they were going to come at me.

That's when I said: Jesus. And immediately in the place where I was—the room or the dimension—there was a hole at the top. Something broke... it was as if there had been an explosion on the roof, and then I saw an army coming dressed all in white; with white horses. They chased Satan and his army out.

At the head of this army from above, there was someone dressed all in white. I couldn't see her face. I couldn't see the faces of the people dressed in white. I could see that they were dressed in white and that there was light on their faces. For the others, it was nothing but black on their faces.

The one who had more light than the others was certainly Jesus. For He was in the midst of those who were dressed in white. He chased Satan's army away.

Afterward, I thanked him.

And he said to me: You can love things, but you can't love them more than me.

At the time, I was a bit young and I said to myself, "Well, that makes sense; I'm going to like things, but I'm going to like Jesus more and more." But when you get older... I see that the message He gave me was a warning for the things that were going to come right now.

With all the distractions in the world and all the things the enemy is trying to put on us, there is always someone who wants to play with you, go out with you. All the time, new games; all the time, new shows; lots of things that will make you waste time that you have to spend with God to read, for example, your Bible.

You want to read your Bible. Someone is calling you outside; you want to read your Bible. A new show is here. You want to pray... And here are friends calling you. There are lots of distractions.

When you think about it once, you say to yourself: "OK, it makes sense, we will love Jesus more all the time", but in fact, when we look at our daily lives, we can sadly note that even if We say we love Jesus more than anything... If we love something, we will surely do it all the time and a lot. Even if others tell us not to do it, we are going to do it. That's what I noticed with things.

The message was important and should not be taken lightly,

because you may believe that Jesus is at the center of your life, but in fact, it may be the last thing that comes to mind. Because when you wake up, most of the time, what are you going to say? You wake up, you pick up your phone instead of thanking God, for example. After that, you will surely say to yourself in the middle of the day: "Ha, I forgot to say it in the morning." If you forget something this important, it means that Jesus is not at the center of your life, so you have to be careful.

In this kind of situation, all you have to do is pray, pray, and ask God to help you, because alone, you will never be able to have a relationship with Him; it is impossible; you will have to ask Him for help, and that's it.

And what has changed is that even I have problems like this happen to me. I am not perfect. I am like everyone else, even me sometimes. It's human not to want to read your Bible, it's human not to want to pray, let's say it like that. But it is precisely necessary to do it. So you have to ask God for help.

It's complicated, there are people who will say to themselves: "Oh, it's good, I'm young... It doesn't matter... I don't have my Bible".

But there is no age for that. Having a relationship with God does not interfere with a person's life. For example, he called Samuel when he was about 5 years old. That's why you should always pray, pray; stay on guard. And of course, asking God for help, so that he is at the center of our lives. Because with all the things that are out there right now, very few people have Jesus at number 1.

And it's a message that I think it's not right for me to say to myself, but to everyone; because we is in a generation where a lot of distractions have happened. And there are a lot of Christians who spend less time with Jesus because of all of this. And in their heads, they're going to say again, Jesus is at number 1, but in fact he may be at number 10. So you really have to pray, fast, a lot of things, because right now, we are seeing a lot of things that are happening. And later, it's going to be worse, with all the things that are happening: the new artificial intelligence, which will create lots of new things that will make us forget about God. And it's serious; and it's dangerous, nonetheless. That's what I wanted to testify to.

I also want to say that the name of Jesus is powerful. Because of course, when the enemy attacks you, you're powerless; you're just a man. But they are a power. I testify to remind us that when you say the name of Jesus, something happens in the spiritual realm. When you say "Jesus," you are applying great force, which can put an end to the work of the enemy.

For example, I said "Jesus"... Boom, He appeared, and the others disappeared. That is why we must learn the importance of the name of Jesus, and not neglect it. And that's what I wanted to share in my testimony.

I am trying to keep putting Jesus at number 1. It's not easy, but you have to pray and fast, as I said, and obviously, over time, you'll end up with Jesus at number 1, but it's not easy, you have to keep praying and fasting. Even you can pray with a brother, to make it easier, and that's my testimony, I hope it has helped you.

5

Prayers of consecration and authority

Prayer against spiritual husbands and wives

In the name of Jesus Christ, Son of the Living God, I am speaking to you, spiritual husbands and wives, evil spirits. Have you not heard of the terrible judgment that the Lord rendered when some fallen angels took wives from among the daughters of men?

In the name of Jesus Christ, Son of the Living God—I am speaking to you, spiritual husbands and wives, evil spirits, your end has been decreed in our God, an appalling destruction is coming upon you, upon your offspring, and upon all your kingdoms. (Genesis 6:13)

The Lord is bringing down upon you your plans to make my life a calamity, a desert, and a heap of filth (Psalm 7:15). I command you to leave my life in the name of Jesus.

Spiritual husbands and wives, unclean spirits, marriage between a son or daughter of a man and a spirit is an abomination in the eyes of the Lord. It cuts you out of my life, my home, and my family (Leviticus 18:29). LEAVE in the name of Jesus. GET AWAY from my life, my home, and my family.

Jesus Christ, Son of the Living God, participated in the blood and flesh to annihilate the devil by dying on the cross. He delivered my life from servitude (Hebrews 2:14–15). The person you recognize as your son, daughter, husband, or wife no longer exists. Indeed, I was crucified with Christ. I died to belong to someone else (Galatians 2:20; Romans 7:4).

In the name of Jesus Christ, Son of the Living God, I break down your altars; I break your statues and idols (Deuteronomy 7:5). Jesus said that you cannot harm me (Luke 10:19). The fire of the Holy Spirit is destroying everything you have planted in my life, my home, and my family. Fire consumes every pact and alliance. The spiritual marriage that bound me to you is dissolved. I'm giving up on you and giving you everything you've brought. I don't want anything from you. LEAVE in the name of Jesus.

The Lord covers me with his feathers. I find refuge under his wings, his fidelity is a shield and a breastplate. In the name of Jesus, the terrors of the night, the plague that walks in the darkness, and even the arrows of the day are forever banished from my life (Psalm 91:4–5). I go to bed, and I fall asleep; I wake up, for the Lord is my support (Psalm 3:5).

In the name of Jesus Christ, Son of the Living God, I speak to you, spiritual husbands and wives, evil spirits, you leave and you don't come back. The arrows of the Lord pierce you; the terrors of God line up against you (Job 6:4). The God of heaven extends his bow, and has set you as the aim of his arrows (Lamentations 3:12-13). You are not resisting. Go in the name of Jesus; go away.

Jesus Christ, the Son of the living God, is the Mighty Savior who has been raised up for us. Jesus delivered me from your hands to serve Him without fear and to walk before Him in holiness and justice every day of my life (Luke 1:69–75).

In the name of Jesus Christ, by the power of the Holy Spirit, I send fire upon you : you are slaughtered, you are overthrown, you are snatched up. The powerful angels of My God are completely annihilating you. Fire, fire, fire,... (2 to 3 minutes)

In the name of Jesus, I am resuming my life. I am taking back my star and my wealth. Nothing that you have placed in me remains hidden.

Note: Some people who have a ring will start to feel a burn on their finger — pull on the finger in question as you would remove a normal ring. Do the same for other jewelry placed on other parts of the body (crown at the head, bracelets on the wrists, chains on the neck, hip, or ankle, etc.).

Prayer against the spirits of witchcraft

Father, in the name of Jesus Christ, I renounce all forms of alliance with the devil. I specifically renounce witchcraft, magic, and conscious or unconscious occultism.

Father, I thank you for Jesus, who participated in flesh and blood to become my perfect representative. By his death, Jesus annihilated the one who has the power of death. Satan, you cannot rule where the glorious name of Jesus is exalted. You cannot enslave the one who has made a covenant with the Lord of Glory, Jesus (Hebrews 2 verse 14).

Woe to you, spirits of witchcraft! Woe to you, sorcerers! The Lord has turned his face against you. Do you think you will surprise the souls of those who are called by his name and keep your peace ? No, there will be no peace for you (Ezekiel 13 verse 18).

The Lord hits you on the cheek, he breaks your teeth (Psalm 3:7). Your manipulations and shenanigans lead to your own downfall (Psalm 5 verse 10). Spirit of sorcery, in the name of Jesus, you retreat, you falter, you perish before the face of my God (Psalm 9 verse 3).

Your enchantments and curses are broken in the name of Jesus. What you have placed in my body and in my life is broken, completely destroyed. The Lord sends fire and hail, snow and fog, and strong winds against you (Psalm 148 verse 8). You are slaughtered, knocked down, and plucked up (Jeremiah 1 verse

10).

Spirits of witchcraft, you cannot hide from the face of My God. You are naked and exposed in front of her face. He ruled in my favor: free my life and go. LEAVE in the name of Jesus.

Fire, lightning, and thunder are coming down on you right now. Leave my life in the name of Jesus. Your chains on my neck are broken. Your chains on my hands are broken. Your chains on my feet are broken. Your chains on my hip are broken.

All of your means of control placed anywhere in my body are destroyed in the name of Jesus.

Spirits of witchcraft, Jesus Christ completely annihilated you at the Cross. Your certain end is the burning lake of fire and brimstone. Jesus said you could not harm me. In the name of Jesus, I declare: There will be no premature death in my home and in my family.

Father, may your fire burn with strength throughout my be-ing. It is fire that purifies. It is fire that destroys the works of witchcraft. Holy Spirit breaks all resistance. May every influence of witchcraft be eradicated, along with its network of demons, in the name of Jesus. Let the fire of the Holy Spirit destroy you. Fire, fire, fire...

In the name of Jesus, the altars of witchcraft, the high places of witchcraft, your airports, your communication equipment, and everything you have established in my life, my home, and my family are completely destroyed. (2 Chronicles 28 verse 4).

Spirit of sorcery, the Lord rains coals, fire, and brimstone on you. A burning wind is the chalice that you share (Psalm 11 verses 2 and 6). No, you cannot continue to remain in my life. No, you cannot continue to oppress. No, you can't keep trapping souls. My life belongs to Jesus. Leave now, go away. You are banned forever.

Your kingdom is being ransacked and completely destroyed by the angels of my God. The doors of your prisons are broken. The captives are freed as I speak in the name of Jesus. The wealth you stole has been returned to its owners.

Prayer against thieves of stars and wealth

In the name of Jesus Christ, I send the destroying wind against all those who have come to steal my riches (Jeremiah 51 verse 1); they rely on you everywhere to execute the judgment of the Lord who condemned you.

Give back, in the name of Jesus : return the star, return everything you have taken, return the money, return the marriage, return the children, restore the peace, restore the joy, restore the promotion, restore health, restore vision, restore prosperity, etc.

The armies of our God stretch their bows against you sorcerers, the armies of our God stretch their bows against you demons : you are wounded to death; you are pierced (Jeremiah 51 verses

3 to 4).

The Lord of heavenly hosts is with me, I am not abandoned (Jeremiah 51 verse 5).

It is the time of our God's revenge — he repays you according to your works. You drink the wine of his wrath; you are delirious (Jeremiah 51 verse 7)

In the name of Jesus Christ, out of my life—give back and go. I'm kicking you out, Go away. My life is the temple of the Holy Spirit, leave in the name of Jesus.

In the name of Jesus, you are broken; you all fall — your chastisement reaches to heaven and rises to the clouds (Jeremiah 51 verse 9).

The Lord shows the justice of our cause: hallelujah, he has set me free; I am sanctified (Jeremiah 51 verse 10).

The Lord has made a resolution against you — sorcerers and demons. And he is carrying out what he said against you. You are slaughtered, you are knocked down, you are ripped off (Jeremiah 1 verse 10).

I raise the banner of the Lord against you — sorcerers and demons. I walk on you in the name of Jesus. (Jeremiah 51 verse 12)

The armies of our God are crying out for war against you: sorcerers and demons. You fall under their domination. In the name of Jesus, restore and go (Jeremiah 51 verse 14).

The Lord sends his hammer of destruction upon you: it breaks and trashes. There is no peace for the villains and rebels that you are.

The Lord extends his hand over you; he rolls you off the rocks; he finds you in your last entrenchments, his fire ignites you (Jeremiah 51 verse 25).

Your kingdoms are devastated: no cornerstones or foundation stones will be shot at your home ; for your homes are completely destroyed. Our God is making you a heap of ruins (Jeremiah 51 verse 26).

In the name of Jesus Christ, the earth shakes, it trembles; for the Lord's plan against you is fulfilled; he makes your kingdoms and homes a desert without inhabitants (Jeremiah 51 verse 29).

The Lord defends my cause; his wrath falls on you, destroyers. In the name of Jesus, restore and go (Jeremiah 51 verse 36).

Prayer to destroy the altar of infertility

Father, I thank you for Jesus, who participated in flesh and blood. By his death, he destroyed the power of the devil. He has broken the chains of servitude. I am delivered (Hebrews 2 verses 14 to 15).

Jesus became sinful in my place so that I could become the righteousness of God. No one can condemn me (2 Corinthians 5 Verse 21).

Infertility altars that speak against my life, hear the voice of the Lord: It is enough to have brought calamity and desolation. You are destroyed; you are ruined; you are destroyed and uprooted (Jeremiah 1:10).

The Lord has established me as a strong city, an iron column, and a brass wall against you. He is with me to deliver me (Jeremiah 1 verses 18 to 19). In the name of Jesus, you disappear. You are troubled by the fire of the Lord, you demons and sorcerers who use these altars. Out of my life.

The armies of our God are raising war cries against you: infertility altars, sorcerers, demons, and mystical animals. You fall under their domination. You are destroyed (Jeremiah 51:14).

The covenants and pacts on which you rely are void; the person you lay charges against died on the cross to belong to another (Romans 7:4). I am the property of Jesus. I rebuke you in the name of Jesus. I am commanding you to leave my life now (Luke 10:19).

The Lord punishes your transgressions severely. He hits you, infertility altars. You are broken. You fall to the ground, and you are never beaten up again (Amos 3:14).

Whom the Lord has blessed, you cannot curse. I am fruitful, I multiply and fill the earth, I subdue it; and I dominate (Genesis

1 verse 28).

Spirit of infertility, the Lord promulgated it, and his decree will not be repealed: there shall not be male or female barren among you, or among your cattle. (Deuteronomy 7:14).

Because of the covenant, the Lord turned to me and made me fruitful—I will multiply (Leviticus 26 verse 9). Retire, impure spirits! Withdraw in the name of Jesus — take away everything you have sown in my life.

No, you can't. Your reign has come to an end. The Lamb of God was slaughtered. He paid my debt. There is no legal ground you are relying on (Romans 12 verse 1). In the name of Jesus, go away.

The Lord is threatening you, spirit of infertility. There will be no peace for you or for those in your kingdom. You will no longer destroy the fruits of my life (Malachi 3:11).

I enjoy the work of my hands. I am happy and thriving. I am a fruitful vine inside my house. My sons are like olive plants around my table. Indeed, the Lord has blessed me infinitely in Jesus Christ (Psalm 128 verses 2-4).

The waters of the Lord flow in abundance in my body and my life. Any trash you have dropped off is taken away. All disabilities are healed. My body is working perfectly. I am fruitful and full of branches (Ezekiel 19 verse 10).

The Lord brought me back from captivity. I left your spiritual prisons with my star and all my possessions. The Lord has given me deliverance, healing, and health (Jeremiah 33 verses 6 to 7). Hallelujah.

Prayer to destroy all infirmity

Father, in the name of Jesus, I praise you for who you are. You are merciful and compassionate, slow to anger, and rich in kindness and faithfulness. You keep your love for up to a thousand generations. Through Jesus Christ, you forgave my iniquity, rebellion, and sin; you delivered me from the iniquity of my father's house (Exodus 34 verses 6 to 7).

Because of the sacrifice of the Cross, You have promulgated the decree that no infirmity or disease will strike me because I belong to you. You are the Lord who heals me (Exodus 15:26).

Spirit of infirmity, I speak to you in the name of Jesus. At the Cross, the Lamb of God took on my disabilities; he took care of my diseases. As his hand touches my body and his voice sounds, you are devastated. His word is driving you out of my life. Leave and never come back again (Matthew 8 verses 15 to 17).

By the power of the Holy Spirit, in the name of Jesus, I decree: The fire goes out on all your altars. They are knocked down. They won't talk against anyone anymore. The Lord is putting you under my feet. Out of my life. Out of my life in the name of Jesus (Malachi 1 verse 10; Luke 10 verse 19).

Spirit of infirmity, your reign is over. The Holy Spirit covers me with its shadow. The oil is poured abundantly all over my being. Everything that you have planted in me has been neutralized and completely destroyed. All mystical poison, all mystical animals, and the fruits of manipulations and shenanigans are removed from my life and my body. Go in the name of Jesus (Mark 6 verse 13).

I am raising the name of Jesus above my life. I put my trust in the work of the cross. I am completely free from all oppression. The life of God drives away all pain and infirmity. All members of my body are strengthened (Acts 3 verse 16).

Spirit of infirmity, I speak to you in the name of Jesus: do you not know that my body is the temple of the Holy Spirit? And that I was redeemed at the price of his blood? Do you not know that I belong to the Lord of all spirits?

Prayer against oppression

Father, in the name of Jesus, I praise you for knowing me before the foundation of the world. You wanted me. It was for your glory that you created me. Your love for me is infinitely great (Jeremiah 1 verse 5).

Father, you have seen my pain. You have heard my cries and you have seen my pain (Exodus 3 verse 7).

I renounce all anger, all bitterness, and all resentment against You, O my God, and against anyone. I decided to forgive the person who hurt me. I decided to bless the person who offended me.

In the name of Jesus, through the power of the Holy Spirit, I break the chains of my oppressors. Spirits of oppression, you fall under my power in the name of Jesus. Jesus gave me the authority to walk on you. You are bound, you are defeated, you are overthrown — I rule you in the name of Jesus (Isaiah 14 verse 2).

The Lord has declared it: your oppression is broken. I enter into God's rest in the name of Jesus (Isaiah 14 verses 3 to 4).

Spirits that have troubled my life, home, and family, you are now relentlessly pursued by the mighty angels of my God. There will be no peace for you. The stick of the villain and the rod of the dominator are broken. Your reign is over. You won't hit anyone anymore. You will no longer subjugate anyone in the name of Jesus (Isaiah 14 verses 5 to 6).

Spirits who oppressed my life, my home, and my family, I speak to you in the name of Jesus: be thrown into the abyss of darkness. You are devastated. You are powerless. Jesus Christ has robbed you. (Isaiah 14 verse 10; Hebrews 2 verse 14; Colossians 2 verses 14 to 15)

In the name of Jesus, all fall, oppressive spirits. You are brought down to the ground and you go down into the abyss (Isaiah 14 verse 12).

You are being expelled from my life. You disappear from all places which are under my administration. The Lord annihilates your council. You are in confusion (Isaiah 19 verse 3). LEAVE in the name of Jesus.

The Lord of the heavenly hosts has poured out a spirit of vertigo on you and you are in confusion and desolation. LEAVE in the name of Jesus. Get out of my life; get out of my house; get out of my family.

Unclean spirits, the Lord has taken a resolution against you. His powerful hand is agitating to destroy you (Isaiah 19 verses 16-17).

It was in Jesus that he recreated me. What can you really do against the one he picked? He called me by name; he blessed me with all kinds of spiritual blessings in heavenly places; he multiplied me. He issued the decree: joy and gladness shall be found therein, thanksgiving, and the voice of melody. (Isaiah 51 verses 2 to 3).

Spirits that oppressed my life, my home, and my family. The Lord is judging you. You're drinking the cup of dizziness; you drink the cup of his anger. Out of my life in the name of Jesus.

Put back everything you have taken. Put everything back in the name of Jesus.

Prayer to cancel covenants and pacts

I break and cancel all the ungodly covenants, oaths, and commitments that I have made with my lips in the name of Jesus.

I renounce and break all the oaths made by my ancestors to false gods, idols, demons, false religions or impious people. I declare the pacts and covenants on which it was based null and void. In the name of Jesus (Matthew 5 verse 33).

I break and cancel all covenants with death and hell made by my ancestors in the name of Jesus.

I break and cancel all ungodly covenants made with idols or demons by my ancestors in the name of Jesus (Exodus 23 Verse 32).

I break and cancel all blood covenants made by sacrifice that would affect my life in the name of Jesus.

Because of the sacrifice of the Cross, I declare null and void all the covenants and pacts that gave Satan any access to my life. With the blood of Jesus, I seal the doors of my life and my home.

In the name of Jesus, I break and cancel every covenant made through the occult, magic, and witchcraft. I was crucified at the Cross to belong to someone else. Jesus is the owner of my life. I am a new creature.

I am breaking and canceling all spiritual marriages entered into with or without my consent. I banish spiritual husbands and wives from my life. Leave my life in the name of Jesus. Your reign is over.

I declare null and void any alliance, any marriage, any association with any demon. You will no longer pollute my life. LEAVE in the name of Jesus.

I am breaking all agreements with hell in the name of Jesus (Isaiah 28 verse 18). I am breaking all alliances with the Kingdom of Waters. I am breaking all alliance with the Kingdom of Mountains or Forests. I am breaking all covenants with all the Realms of the Devil. You're leaving my life right now. Jesus gave me the authority to walk on you. I'm crushing you. Leave without delay — in the name of Jesus.

I have a covenant with God through the blood of Jesus Christ. I am united with the Lord and am one spirit with him. I am breaking all ungodly covenants and renewing my covenant with God through the body and blood of Jesus.

I separate myself from any demon who could take my life through ancestral covenants in the name of Jesus.

I bind and drive out any family demon (or familiar spirit) who would follow my life through ancient alliances in the name of Jesus.

I give you back your titles, your gifts, your rings, your chains, and your clothes. In the name of Jesus, I consume them with the fire of the Holy Spirit. Grab your things, get them out of my life right away. You are shot, you are knocked down, and you are ripped off.

Prayer to establish the blessing

Father, in the name of Jesus, I praise You for the Covenant made between You and Jesus Christ, my representative. I praise you because, by recreating me in Him, you have made me a partaker of your life.

I have been crucified with Christ. If I live, it is no longer me who lives, it is Christ who lives in me. No, he did not come in part; he is present in me with all his glory, all his majesty, and all his power. All that is in God dwells within me. (Galatians 2 verse 20, Colossians 2 verse 10)

I like your presence. I take pleasure in your word. I hasten to put into practice the instructions given to me by your glorious Spirit. You are My God. It is for You that I live (2 Corinthians 5 verses 14 to 15).

I am listening to the voice of your Spirit. It leads me on the path of justice. It gives me superiority over my competitors and enemies. (Deuteronomy 28 verse 1).

I am blessed wherever I live. I am blessed in all that I do (Deuteronomy 28 verse 3). The fruit of my womb, the fruit of every step I take in any area of my life, is blessed (Deuteronomy

28 verse 4).

My basket and my hutch are blessed. What comes into my hands multiplies. Nothing is lost (Deuteronomy 28 verse 4).

The Lord commanded the blessing to be with me. His favor accompanies me everywhere I go and in everything I do.

People fear me because they see in what ways the Lord has favored me. The sky is open over my life. And the blessings of the Lord flow like a stream through me. I lend to a lot and I don't borrow myself.

I love the Lord with all my heart, soul, thoughts, and strength (Deuteronomy 6 verses 4-5). I hold His word in my heart. She is Spirit and Life. It transports me to the heights of its glory. I am at the top, not at the bottom. I am the head and not the tail (Deuteronomy 28:13).

The Word of the Lord is the truth. She created all things. I hold fast to your word in my heart. She establishes the rule of God in all areas of my life.

Jesus paid my debt. I am a participant in the life of God. I am one spirit with My Lord. As it is now, that's the way I am. I don't lack anything because he ordered the Blessing to fill me up.

I am filled with all sorts of spiritual blessings in Jesus. They are brought into being through the power of His Spirit. They are brought into being through the power of His Spirit.

Prayer to assert our dominance

Father, You have established your throne above the heavens and your kingdom extends over all things (Psalm 103 verse 19).

Forever, your word endures in heaven. From generation to generation, your loyalty endures. You founded the earth and it stands firm (Psalm 119 verses 89 to 90).

I thank you because you have blessed me with all kinds of spiritual blessings in heavenly places in Jesus Christ (Ephesians 1 verse 3).

You elected me before the foundation of the world to be holy and blameless before your face (Ephesians 1 verse 4).

You have made known to me the mystery of your will: I am one spirit with Jesus Christ (Ephesians 1 verses 9-10; 1 Corinthians 6 verse 17).

The Spirit of God lives in me. I have God's wisdom and intelligence. I have God's advice and strength. I have the knowledge and piety of God. I am also filled with the fear of God (Isaiah 11 verse 2).

Since I have become united with him in the likeness of his death, I will also be part of his resurrection (Romans 6 verses 4 to 5).

I am sitting with Jesus in the highest places (Ephesians 2 verse 6). In Jesus, I am above all dominion, above all authority, above all power, above all dignity, and above every name that can be called, not only in the present age, but also in the age to come (Ephesians 1:21).

In the name of Jesus, I am speaking to those of you who think you can rule over my life. The Lord put everything under the feet of Jesus, and made Him the head of the Church, which is his body. In Jesus, the fullness of God dwells (Ephesians 1 verse 22). Your fight against his designs in my life is in vain. I rebuke you in the name of Jesus.

No, you can't. You are under his feet. On the cross, he completely robbed you. You fall under my power. There will be no peace for you. Leave my life in the name of Jesus. LEAVE now.

In the past, I was unaware of the power of the Cross. Today, I know. He paid my debt. The Father charged him with my sin and iniquity. After three days in Hell, he fully satisfied the requirements of God's justice. Hallelujah.

I have been redeemed through His blood. I have received adoption; I am no longer a slave to the rudiments of the world. I am a child of God. Your manipulations and shenanigans do not affect me. Because he said you couldn't hurt me.

I rely on the perfect justice of Jesus. Through his act of obedience, he made me a part of the life of God. The reign of death and sin is over. The grace and justice of God rule in all areas of life.

It will be with my life, as he said. I condemn your words, which were a judgment against my life. There is no longer any legal ground. How will you accuse he who is one spirit with the Lord of the Lords and the King of Kings?

The Lord reigns forever. He ruled in my favor. I am free from all charges, and I am free from all debt. I don't participate in the table of demons. My star and my wealth are kept in Jesus.

Becoming a Christian

Simple and clear conditions for all men.

God has clearly established the conditions for moving from Lucifer's dominion to fellowship with God.

Acts 2:37-41; KJV

"37 Now when they heard this, they were pricked in their heart, and said unto Peter and to the rest of the apostles, Men and brethren, what shall we do? 38 Then Peter said unto them, Repent, and be baptized every one of you in the name of Jesus Christ for the remission of sins, and ye shall receive the gift of the Holy Ghost. 39 For the promise is unto you, and to your children, and to all that are afar off, even as many as the Lord our God shall call. 40 And with many other words did he testify and exhort, saying, Save yourselves from this untoward generation. 41 Then they that gladly received his word were baptized: and the same day there were added unto them about three thousand souls."

On the day the Church was established in Jerusalem, Peter proclaimed the death and resurrection of Jesus as God's offer of salvation to all people.

A large crowd came from several provinces to celebrate the feast of Pentecost. The speech deeply stirred them, prompting a question that remains of great interest to us: "Brethren, what shall we do?" verse 37 — It goes back to the question we are trying to answer in this section: "How do you become a Christian?" "

Step 1: The gospel of Christ needs to be preached.

Romans 3 verses 9–11; KJV

9 What then? are we better than they? No, in no wise: for we have before proved both Jews and Gentiles, that they are all under sin; 10 As it is written, There is none righteous, no, not one: 11 There is none that understandeth, there is none that seeketh after God.

Romans 3 verse 23 ; KJV

For all have sinned, and come short of the glory of God;

> ***Romans 6 verse 23 ; KJV***
>
> *For the wages of sin is death, but the gift of God is eternal life through Jesus Christ our Lord.*

> ***John 3 verse 16; KJV***
>
> *For God so loved the world, that he gave his only begotten Son, that whosoever believeth in him should not perish, but have everlasting life.*

Jesus died and rose again for the benefit of those who believe.

Step 2: The man must repent

This is Pierre's response to those who wanted to know what to do.

Repentance means recognizing God's diagnosis of the situation and making the decision to give up on leading our lives in our own ways. He who repents comes down from the throne of his life. He surrendered to Jesus Christ, who died on the cross in his place.

From that moment on, he declared himself dead to his former life because he recognized that he died in Jesus on the cross. And he recognizes that he has risen in Jesus for new life.

Jesus said, "If anyone wants to be my disciple, let him deny himself..."

This stage is crucial because the death of the old nature is necessary for the new creation to appear.

Churches are full of people who have never done this step properly. They claim the name Christian, but they are leading their lives according to their old nature. Now the Scriptures declare that he who is in Christ is a new creation, the old things have passed away, and behold, all things have become new.

Individuals who earnestly adhere to this path experience a transformation in their spirit through the Spirit of God.

John 1 verses 12–13; KJV

12 But as many as received him, to them gave he power to become the sons of God, even to them that believe on his name: 13 Which were born, not of blood, nor of the will of the flesh, nor of the will of man, but of God.

God recreates the spirit of every person who heartily receives the gospel of Christ and who completes the repentance stage correctly.

Step 3: Immersion in water

Jesus Christ gave the ordinance of immersion in water to fulfill all the righteousness of God in the believer's life. It is the convert who is immersed so that the seal may be placed on his conscious commitment to follow Jesus Christ. He is made a partaker in the benefits of the death and resurrection of Jesus Christ.

Water immersion should normally immediately follow the repentance or conversion stage.

Step 4: Immersion in the Holy Spirit

The Christian is called in the manner of Christ. It is configured according to the model that descends from the sky. Thus, Jesus requires that he follow the steps that he has established.

Immersion in the Holy Spirit is the coming into the recreated spirit of the new convert of the Spirit of God. He receives the One who will lead and equip him for the fulfillment of his mission.

No one is called to do God's work by natural means. The Church of Jesus is d to the armies of Lucifer. We need power from above to establish the kingdom of our God.

About the Author

Yves Djiki is a minister of the Word of God. Driven by the Holy Spirit, he dedicated more than two decades to studying and imparting the teachings of Jesus: the tenets of the kingdom of God, healing, deliverance, among others.

Along with his wife Bénédicte, Yves runs the Vie Pour Christ Church, which they founded in 2012 with a focus on producing end-time disciples. An extension of this work has existed in Cameroon since 2020.

They share their passion for the scriptures through the ImmersionRhema meditation framework (https://immersionrhema.com/), which is changing lives around the world.

Yves, Bénédicte and their children live in Montreal, Canada.

You can connect with me on:

- https://amazon.com/author/yvesdjiki
- https://x.com/ysdjiki
- https://bit.ly/3VIJB4R
- https://www.tiktok.com/@ysdjiki
- https://www.youtube.com/@EgliseViePourChrist
- https://www.facebook.com/EgliseViepourChrist
- https://www.instagram.com/egliseviepourchrist
- https://www.tiktok.com/@egliseviepourchrist?lang=en